The Cathedrals, Abbeys & Priories of Wales

Cathedral Builders

They climbed on sketchy ladders towards God,
With winch and pulley hoisted hewn rock into heaven,
Inhabited sky with hammers, defied gravity,
Deified stone, took up God's house to meet him,

And came down to their suppers and small beer;
Every night slept, lay with their smelly wives,
Quarrelled and cuffed the children, lied,
Spat, sang, were happy or unhappy,

And every day took to the ladders again;
Impeded the rights of way of another summer's
Swallows, grew greyer, shakier, became less inclined
To fix a neighbour's roof of a fine evening,

Saw naves sprout arches, clerestories soar,
Cursed the loud fancy glaziers for their look,
Somehow escaped the plague, got rheumatism,
Decided it was time to give it up,

To leave the spire to others; stood in the crowd
Well back from the vestments at the consecration,
Envied the fat bishop his warm boots,
Cocked up a squint eye and said, 'I bloody did that.'

John Ormond

The Cathedrals, Abbeys & Priories of Wales

by
Tim McCormick

Logaston Press

LOGASTON PRESS
Little Logaston Woonton Almeley
Herefordshire HR3 6QH
logastonpress.co.uk

First published by Logaston Press 2010
Copyright text © Tim McCormick 2010
Copyright illustrations © Tim McCormick except as otherwise acknowledged 2010

ISBN 978 1 906663 29 2

Typeset by Logaston Press
and printed in Great Britain by
Bell & Bain Ltd., Glasgow

Cover illustrations clockwise from top left:
South transept, Ewenny (Malcolm Thurlby); Llanthony (Malcolm Thurlby);
Valle Crucis (Logaston Press); Llandaff Cathedral (Logaston Press);
Margam Abbey; the new cloisters at St Davids Cathedral

Contents

Acknowledgements

The author would like to thank the Deans and Chapters of the six Church in Wales cathedrals for giving permission to photograph the interiors of their churches. Thank you to Nevil James, hon. Archivist of Llandaff Cathedral, for supplying information about the sedilia fragments. Thanks also to Christopher Davies (Publishers) Ltd for giving permission to reproduce John Ormond's poem 'Cathedral Builders' from his collection *Requiem and Celebration*. Thank you to Claire Reeves and The National Trust for supplying the picture used for the rear cover. And not least, to Peter McCormick for his sympathetic photography and processing.

Introduction

This book is concerned chiefly with medieval religious architecture. Both the methods of building construction and the monastic Orders are discussed in some detail, to help the reader to gain a fuller appreciation of the diverse styles and functions of the buildings themselves. After the Norman Conquest the architectural styles of Britain during succeeding eras diffused and developed as a whole, although of course distinct regional stylistic characteristics can be discerned in a number of instances. If one looks at the architecture of Wales generally during the period, the main characteristic compared with that of England is the modesty of scale. Wales was a much poorer country, a regional and troubled outpost which received a far lower level of patronage than did England, and if in Wales we find no Winchester, no Durham, and no Wells, it is also true that the quality of what can be seen begs for no allowances at all. There is no equivalent in England of the nave of St Davids. Its pulpitum, cathedra and Holy Trinity Chapel are of the first rank. Brecon contains some of the finest Early English architecture anywhere. Llandaff's Norman arches are unsurpassed. And Penmon can boast an authentic Norman spire of which it would be hard to find a counterpart in England. The famous monastic ruins of Fountains and Rievaulx are equalled if not surpassed in beauty (and indeed importance) at Margam and Tintern, and Newport and Llandaff display notable examples of modern architecture amidst the medieval work.

It seems paradoxical that the religious Orders, dedicated initially at least as they were to the ideals of poverty and austere ways of living, should have been the instigators of some of the most aesthetically beautiful buildings that the world has seen. R.S. Thomas wrote, 'We have over-fashioned our faith. Our churches are as limousines in the procession towards heaven.' Well yes! The great church was indeed intended to give a glimpse of heaven on earth to all those who entered, and no expense was spared. But as far as the monks and nuns were concerned they were building to the glory of God. The benefactors were too, buying themselves places in heaven, but there were other considerations such as personal and political status which urged them to spare no expense. The master mason also built to the glory of God, and it was the chief means by which he and his colleagues could prosecute their crafts and artistic skills. The church was far and away the most important patron of the arts in the Middle Ages, and one sometimes wonders what legacy we would have had if the church had remained aloof from material display. What would have replaced St Davids, Brecon and Tintern as vehicles for artistic expression? The unskilled labourer also built to the glory of God, and thoughts should be spared for him.

Accidents and even fatalities among the master craftsmen were not unknown, but it was the sweat and toil of the ordinary common man that brought these buildings into being; it was sometimes at the cost of his health, and sometimes at the cost of his life. He worked for most of the daylight hours, and in the winter months, when it became too cold to set stone, he was laid off.

This book should be useful for any lover and student of the architecture of the period in general, and hopefully the examples that come under scrutiny will meet the reader as fresh and even surprising alternatives to those which are usually encountered. The buildings are celebrated in the illustrations, and I am grateful to my brother Peter whose photography quite properly upstages the text.

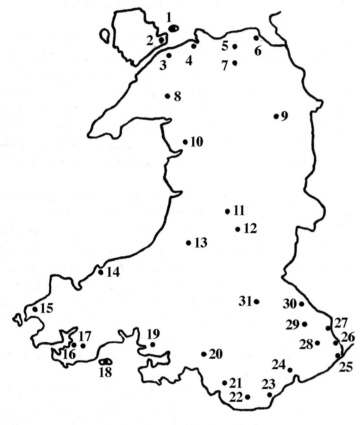

Location of sites mentioned in the text
(Appendix 2 gives essential details of smaller sites not otherwise covered as there are no standing remains)

1. Ynys Seiriol
2. Penmon
3. Bangor
4. Conwy
5. St Asaph
6. Basingwerk
7. Denbigh
8. Beddgelert
9. Valle Crucis
10. Cymer
11. Llanidloes
12. AbbeyCwm-hir
13. Strata Florida
14. St Dogmael's
15. St Davids
16. Monkton
17. Lamphey
18. Caldey
19. Kidwelly
20. Neath
21. Margam
22. Ewenny
23. Llandaff
24. Newport
25. Chepstow
26. Tintern
27. Monmouth
28. Usk
29. Abergavenny
30. Llanthony
31. Brecon

1

Christianity in Wales: a brief introduction

This book is devoted mainly to the building period between the Norman Conquest and the dissolution of the monasteries during Henry VIII's reign. The latter date chooses itself as it is the point at which major religious building projects in stone ceased, even in mid-build in one or two cases: for example the unfinished western tower at Bolton Priory in Yorkshire, whilst the north transept of St Dogmael's church, rebuilt in the early sixteenth century, was presumably meant to be followed by further rebuilding work in the new style before the project was cut short. The former date requires a little more explanation, and a small digression into the pre-Norman architecture of England will help to underline its scarcity in Wales.

There are around two hundred and fifty or so Saxon or part-Saxon buildings identified in England. The constructional details of some Saxon cathedrals have been recovered in great detail, and in the post-Conquest abbey church of Sherborne there are portions of the earlier Saxon cathedral within its fabric. We also know much of Edward the Confessor's Westminster Abbey, which was largely complete by the eve of the Conquest, and we can still see St Paul's church at Jarrow, Tyne and Wear, where the Venerable Bede worshipped. Some early post-Conquest churches also display characteristics both Saxon and Norman, and it is here that it is possible to find an analogy of sorts in Wales where Celtic motifs are sometimes found decorating otherwise overtly Norman and English buildings. But between the Roman occupation and the Norman Conquest, there were no building projects in Wales in stone to compare with those of England.

What are completely missing, however, are the structures the Celts built in timber. Practically all Celtic non-religious (and particularly in Wales, religious also) buildings were built with timber, so either no longer exist or have been replaced in stone. The timber church at Greensted in Essex is a unique survivor and even then dates from a later period — the late eleventh century. But the fact that surviving pre-Conquest stone churches are numerous in England, despite the Norman policy of systematic demolition of Saxon churches to build anew upon their foundations, tells us something in itself about the differing outlooks of the Celtic and Saxon cultures.

The religious movement emanating from Papal Rome, and to which Saxon England was bound, was a centralized, hierarchical one with a large political dimension. It built on a monumental scale, whilst the church-building programme which followed William the

Conqueror's invasion of England was as much a political statement of a conqueror as a religious one.

By contrast, the Celtic church was based upon the spiritual rather than the material, and this development was encouraged by the wars following the withdrawal of the Romans in the fifth century which on the one hand brought about Saxon England, and on the other hand mitigated against permanent settlements and long-term building projects in Wales as the Celts constantly fought both to maintain their independence, and also amongst themselves.

Further differences are illustrated by the reception St Augustine received when he met the bishops of Wales towards the end of the sixth century. Here was a powerful representative of the Catholic church, an emissary of Pope Gregory the Great who presided over a religious empire centred on Rome, and Augustine had come to convert the southern kingdoms of Anglo-Saxon England to Christianity. After a later meeting between Augustine and the Celtic bishops they acknowledged that he was a messenger of truth, and indicated that they would be willing to conform to the usages and practices of his church, but that they could not do so without obtaining the assent of their people. When they next met Augustine, they were much more emphatic in their reply. They expressed an unwillingness to align themselves with Rome and Canterbury just as they had fought to maintain independence from Saxon England, especially since Augustine was emphasizing points of difference on which they must conform to Roman practice, for example the time of Easter, the administration of baptism, and the restrictions to be imposed regarding the preaching of the Gospel to the Saxons. Most importantly, they resented the fact that this man had sought to secure the submission of the Celtic church to Rome; this was an alien concept to the Celtic religious community.

The origins and growth of monasticism and of the related style of the buildings covered here results from the monastic movement that first evolved in Egypt, where some hermits lived alone in huts or caves, others in great communities, which then spread northwards and westwards. Roman Britain had become officially Christian by the edict of Emperor Constantine the Great in the fourth century. In Ireland monasticism flourished, migrating, after the withdrawal of the Romans from Britain, to Wales, Scotland and Cornwall. In 563 St Columba left Ireland to found a Celtic monastery on Iona, and the Celtic church then spread to Northumbria, St Aidan establishing a monastery at Lindisfarne. Isolated locations (congenial to a life of religious contemplation) were deliberately sought, and the remains of the Celtic monastery on Ynys Seiriol (Puffin Island) off the east coast of Anglesey is a north-western European equivalent to the eastern deserts chosen by the monastic movement's founders. St Illtud subsequently founded a monastery at Llaniltud Fawr (Llantwit Major), and Bardsey and Caldey islands also had communities of monks. These latter two sites were also chosen for post-Conquest foundations, and Caldey today has a community of Cistercians.

The sites of early Christian settlements are often indicated by the place name prefix *Llan* (enclosure). Nearly six hundred of these exist in Wales, and the second half of the word is usually the name of the saint associated with the foundation, for example Llan-Illtud, Llan-Idloes. Occasionally, a location is indicated; Llandaff: a settlement by the river Taff.

When Celtic leaders in what became England were forced to emigrate to Brittany as a result of Saxon invasions in the fifth century they took this tradition with them, and numerous place names in Brittany beginning with 'Lan' and 'Tre' have their origins in Britain.

The Celtic/Welsh religious community, or *clas*, would have consisted of a community of both monks and non-monastic clergy under the direction of an abbot (*abad*) who could also be a bishop, but dioceses as we understand the term today were not formed. The bishops and abbots acknowledged no authority above themselves.

Later, Minsters or *clas* churches with canons were established, and these formed the basis for the later parochial system. Solitary and communal monastic ways of living co-existed, and the communal establishments would often prepare a monk for a later phase of travel and solitary contemplation. Samson, for instance, left Llanilltud Fawr to establish a community on Caldey island, and later ones in Cornwall and Brittany. The only visible survivals of some of these foundations, the sites of which have been built and rebuilt upon in successive eras, are the circular churchyards which can sometimes still be seen, and it is notable that Saxon churchyards in England were also circular or curvilinear.

The background to these post-Roman developments were the onslaughts of pagan invaders: Jutes, Angles, Saxons, Picts, and Scots, and it was the three Germanic tribes who eventually created England, and against whom the Celts fought to maintain their independence. The spiritual unity and aspirations of the Celts became the dominant features of their religion, and material preoccupations such as the building of churches in durable materials which would take years of co-ordinated effort to complete, played scant part in their thinking. But their legacy of standing stones and high crosses should not be overlooked. These span the period between the fifth and twelfth centuries; the earliest ones are rough un-dressed slabs of stone onto which are incised crude motifs and religious symbols, but by the end of the Celtic era magnificent high crosses were being produced with a sophistication and quality of craftsmanship which show that it is not only in great buildings that a religious movement can display its virtuosity and vigour.

For the reasons outlined above, actual Celtic monastic remains are scarce, but sufficient examples have been excavated for a good picture of their general characteristics to have been gained. Generally they took the form of a collection of small individual cells grouped around the perimeter walls of a circular or oval enclosure, with very few communal buildings in evidence beyond several chapels and a scriptorium (for writing or copying religious manuscripts). There was no standard plan for the layout of the cells, but the chapel or chapels were placed towards the centre of the enclosure.

Emphasis was on solitary rather than communal living, and the buildings were modest in size. St Seiriol lived during the first half of the sixth century, and the remains of his foundation are to be found on Ynys Seiriol just off the east coast of Anglesey. The oratory, a small chapel for private prayer, was only about five feet square internally.

Indeed the chapels in general tended to be modest, and the semi-circular or apsidal eastern projection, a strong characteristic of Saxon and early Norman architecture, was unknown to the Celtic church. The square east end which became the norm in Britain generally from the mid twelfth century, in contrast to the continuing use of the apsidal east end on the Continent, is perhaps the only example of Celtic architectural influence on the post-

Conquest church. Flat-headed doorways and windows were used rather than arches, and tunnel vaults of stones or pebbles formed the roofs. There are also a number of holy wells in Wales traditionally associated with the early saints, of which Maen-du well in Brecon is a 1754 reconstruction. It gives a good idea of what the Celtic stone buildings looked like, and how they were constructed.

In England the reforms of St Dunstan in the tenth century brought about a more orderly layout of buildings, and the appearance of the cloister around which the other buildings were grouped, together with the adoption of a single church in preference to several chapels, was a reflection of ninth-century developments on the Continent. The Celtic church was isolated from these changes and the ordering of the buildings about a cloister did not appear in Wales until the Normans began their building programme.

The Norman Conquest

Duke William of Normandy's conquest of England in 1066 was comparatively swift. He was able to take advantage of the fact that there were already many ties between England and France, and that in various ways the Normans were already in England. Edward the Confessor's Westminster Abbey, largely complete by 1065, was very much a Norman building as we use the term today, and there are numerous other examples of this architectural overlap during the decades each side of 1066. The Conqueror also made full use of the administrative infrastructure already in place, this being a legacy of King Alfred and his successors from the ninth century onwards as part of the organized defence against Danish invaders. Domesday Book of 1086 is as much a reflection of Saxon organization in the defence of their country as it is of a conqueror's consolidation. The taking over of an administrative system which was already in place was not available to him in Wales, but because the Welsh were not a united people it rendered areas of the country vulnerable to attack from an organized, well-motivated and single-minded invader despite its difficult terrain. During the hundred years or so before the Conquest rivalry between the Welsh rulers was at its height, and at least thirty-five of them are known to have died violently. There were also Viking raids to contend with, and sporadic incursions from Saxon England. The fact that the future King Harold was able to mount a successful campaign into parts of Wales in 1063 gave a clear indication as to the vulnerability of Wales to determined, localized attack.

By 1067, William FitzOsbern was firmly established at Hereford. An important lieutenant of William I, he was given the task of conquering southern Wales. One must appreciate that William I and his followers were well versed in military campaigning, and they were unlikely to tolerate the prospect of independent and hostile flanking territories to the newly conquered England. Complete conquest was their aim; this made sense both in military terms and with respect to bringing about stable political unity in as swift a manner as possible. FitzOsbern established control of the southern border by erecting castles not just at Hereford, but also at Chepstow, Monmouth, Ewyas Harold, Clifford and Wigmore. By the time of his death in 1071 he had penetrated deep into south Wales west of the river Usk.

Further north, invasions were launched from Shrewsbury, led by Roger of Montgomery, and Chester, led by Hugh of Avranches. By the end of the eleventh century it seemed that

Wales was virtually in the hands of William II, but during the last years of the century there were furious uprisings against the Normans throughout Wales. In the north these were relatively successful, but by the end of the century it was clear that the Norman strongholds in the south and east remained largely intact, and the coming to the throne in 1100 of Henry I, a considerable political and military leader, ensured the consolidation of Norman positions. The whole of the southern quarter of Wales, together with small areas along virtually all of the border, an area known collectively as the Marches, came under Anglo-Norman domination, but mid and north-west Wales remained largely autonomous until Edward I's campaigns of the late thirteenth century.

The building programme carried out by the Normans in the decades following the Conquest of England would have been formidable in any age, never mind the eleventh and twelfth centuries. At first, timber castles had to be quickly erected, and some of these were even brought across the Channel in a pre-fabricated state. They were usually replaced by stone structures as quickly as possible, and a massive church building programme was also instigated. A brief list of the larger building projects in hand between the 1070s and the mid twelfth century in England will give an indication of the scale. Churches, either secular or monastic, included St Albans, Battle, Bury St Edmunds, Canterbury, Chester, Durham, Ely, Gloucester, Norwich, Peterborough, Rochester, Selby, Tewkesbury, Worcester, Winchester (begun in 1079 and largely complete by 1100, one of the largest churches in Europe), Carlisle, Chichester, Exeter, Hereford, Lincoln, Sarum and York. The Benedictine monastic Order was a powerful instrument of the political conquest, and in the above list the first fifteen were Benedictine monasteries. Add to this list the building of lesser foundations, the parish churches, the castles, and the continuing campaigns against the Welsh and the Saxon dissenters, and one gets a picture of the scale and determination of Norman activity.

The Normans had no sympathy towards, nor understanding of, the Celtic monastic system in Wales. During the twelfth century it was swept away in south Wales where Anglo-Norman positions were consolidated, and a series of Benedictine houses were established at Abergavenny, Brecon, Chepstow, Kidwelly, Monmouth, Pembroke, and elsewhere. A number of these were daughter houses of English abbeys. Brecon, for instance, belonged to Battle abbey, which had been quickly established adjacent to the site of the Battle of Hastings. By the middle of the twelfth century the four ancient sees of Wales, namely St Davids, Llandaff, Bangor and St Asaph, had been re-founded and their bishops had sworn obedience to Canterbury. But none of these post-Conquest Welsh cathedrals were monastic foundations, whereas many English cathedrals of the period were. Formal territorially defined dioceses were created, and the imposition of the Anglo-Norman pattern in Wales was well under way.

There would now be no distinction between the architecture of England and Wales. The Norman penchant for remorseless organization was reflected in a homogeneity of both church and monastic layout and architectural style throughout Britain, but the style, an importation from the Continent, quite quickly developed peculiar British, and also regional, characteristics. For example, the British favoured long naves and relatively low ceilings and vaults, with substantial central towers over the crossings. The relatively plain exteriors contrasted markedly with Continental counterparts, and this is a particular characteristic of the Welsh cathedrals and abbeys.

In mid and northern Wales where Norman domination was not strong, Celtic-style ornamentation persisted into the thirteenth century, and the twelfth-century nave of Penmon Priory in Anglesey is a remarkable example of a Norman-style church in what was at the time still a Celtic foundation. Celtic decoration can be seen around the south door, and the Augustinian Order did not come here until the thirteenth century.

During the course of the twelfth century the Welsh rulers came to appreciate the methods and tactics of the Anglo-Norman invaders, and to learn from them. They built castles of their own, and themselves began to found monasteries, recognising the importance of the church as a political instrument and ally. The Benedictine Order was a symbol of conquest in the south (there were no Benedictine foundations in Wales north of Brecon) and so the Welsh rulers patronised the Cistercian Order particularly, and also the Augustinian Canons.

Chapters two and three look at both the personalities involved in the church and the development of the monastic Orders during the following centuries in detail.

2

Personalities and Politics in the Welsh Church

This chapter begins with the situation after the Norman invasions of Wales during the years around 1100. The Celtic church had bishops for the four ancient sees of Bangor, St Asaph, Llandaff and St Davids, but there were no formal territorial boundaries and they did not swear allegiance to Rome. Nor was there a parish church organization within each see. The Normans therefore organized the church around the form already recognizable in England, re-founding the ancient sees as territorially defined regions containing a number of parishes and with their bishops swearing allegiance to Canterbury.

Bishop Urban was the first bishop to be appointed to the see of Llandaff in 1107, by Archbishop Anselm of Canterbury. He was a Welsh cleric, and took Urban as the Latinised form of his Welsh name Gwrgan. Anxious to bolster the status of the new diocese, he built the Norman cathedral, parts of which remain, and brought the relics of St Dyfrig from Bardsey island to Llandaff where the remains of St Teilo were already in his keeping. He compiled the *Book of Llandaff*, a collection of charters (some forged), biographies and other documents to demonstrate Llandaff's illustrious history, and also made territorial claims for the diocese which were to be disputed by the bishop of St Davids.

At St Davids, Henry I appointed Bernard in 1115, who paid homage to Henry and swore allegiance to the Archbishop of Canterbury, the latter act a tactical error regarding the prospect of an independent church in Wales. He campaigned for Rome's canonisation of St David, and this was achieved in about 1123. He also campaigned vigorously for the recognition of St Davids as the seat of the archbishop of an autonomous church in Wales, but this foundered with his death in 1148 after it seemed that Rome was at last giving the notion serious consideration.

At Bangor, Hervey le Breton had been appointed in 1092. A chaplain of William Rufus, his relations with the Welsh were so bad that he was forced to travel with an entourage of armed men, and an uprising killed his brother. Forced out of office by Gruffydd ap Cyndn who was leading a Welsh revolt, the see remained vacant until 1120 when David the Scot took office and swore allegiance to Canterbury. He had been master of the cathedral school of Würzburg in Bavaria, and was chosen by Gruffydd ap Gwynedd.

At St Asaph, the Normans appointed Gilbert as their first bishop in 1143, and in 1152 Geoffrey of Monmouth was appointed by Archbishop Theobold. He spent most of his time studying at Oxford in the institution that was to develop into Britain's first university, and it is very unlikely that he ever saw his see. Rebellions led by Owain Gwynedd no doubt contributed to his decision to reside at Oxford. Geoffrey is principally responsible for the legends of Merlin through his book *The Prophecies of Merlin*, and he also wrote a *History of the Kings of Britain* which contains a narrative of the life of King Arthur which he claimed to have translated from ancient Welsh sources, a claim that has not been substantiated. One might forgive a certain lack of disinterested method which one expects of a historian of the modern era, but as far back as 1190 William of Newburgh, an Augustinian canon of Bridlington in Yorkshire, was harshly critical both of Geoffrey's approach to the writing of history and of his tendency to embellish.

Right from these earliest days one sees the trend that was to characterize the Welsh scene to a greater or lesser extent throughout much of the medieval period. On the one hand, the Normans and their successors ostensibly controlled much of Wales and its systems of government, at least in the towns, but it was the Welsh who controlled much of what was happening on the ground. The fact that they were having a say in the appointments even of the earliest bishops demonstrates this, but crucially, all the bishops had sworn their allegiances to Canterbury.

When William the Conqueror defeated King Harold in 1066 he had effectively defeated England, because it was a united country under the rule of a single monarch. That had been William's principal ambition. But when William FitzOsbern defeated the Welsh and founded his monastery and castle at Chepstow soon after the conquest of England, he must have known — just as well as the Welsh princes knew — that his was a local victory. This illustrates both the strength and the weakness of the position of the Welsh princes. On the one hand, Wales was not a united country and therefore to declare any kind of general victory was not possible. In north Wales particularly, the situation with the bishops shows that there existed at best an uneasy truce between the Normans and the Welsh, and it would not be possible for conquest truly to be claimed until Edward I's campaigns a hundred and fifty years later. Wales was a frustrating land with which to deal.

But on the other hand, disunity was a weakness. Rivalry between the Welsh princes had been rife before the twelfth century, and this hardly abated. The disinclination to unite against a common enemy meant that the Principality was vulnerable to attack, and it enabled Wales to be conquered piecemeal over a long period of time. It contributed to Edward I's victories in the thirteenth century, and it also contributed to Owain Glyndŵr's defeat in the fifteenth.

Welsh Foundations

During the twelfth century in south Wales a number of Benedictine houses were established by the Normans, and this Order, with its houses tied to English and French abbeys, was associated with the alien presence of the Norman Marcher lords. The Welsh princes, recognising the value of patronising the church, therefore founded a series of Cistercian houses because that breakaway Order was somewhat less associated with the Normans, its houses not being dependencies of abbeys in England or Normandy. Thus in 1146 AbbeyCwmhir was founded by Maredudd, son of Madog ap Idnerth, and the house was to be established from Whitland Abbey. But Maredudd was killed by the Normans in 1146 and the founding was aborted. In 1176, when The Lord Rhys was controlling much of south-west Wales, Maredudd's son Cadwallon re-founded the abbey at its present site, he and his brother Einion Clud being the chief benefactors. Whitland was originally founded in about 1140 from Clairvaux in France, but The Lord Rhys took control of it and became its patron. Strata Florida, originally founded by Robert FitzStephen in 1164, was again soon re-founded by Rhys on a new site. This abbey had great significance for the Welsh, and a number of Rhys's family were buried there. Rhys also founded Llanllyr in about 1180. Cymer was founded in 1198 by monks from Cwmhir, Maredudd ap Cynan, cousin of Llywelyn the Great, being its benefactor. Llanllugan was founded in about 1200 by Maredudd ap Rhotpert, Lord of Cydewain. In the south-east, which was dominated by the Normans with their Benedictine houses, Cistercian Llantarnam was founded in 1179 by Hywel ap Iorwerth. In the north, Valle Crucis was founded by Madoc ap Gruffydd Maelor, ruler of Powys, in 1201. The Welsh leaders were giving land and resources to the monasteries, putting them out of reach of the invaders, and they appreciated that if they did not found this series of abbeys and take advantage of the control of land and local administration that they exercised, the Anglo-Normans would certainly have done so.

The scene had been set for the next hundred years. Wales was occupied by the Anglo-Normans, but ruled on the ground to a large extent by the Welsh. The Benedictine and some of the earlier Augustinian and Cistercian monasteries were patronised by the invaders, but most of the later Cistercian houses were patronised by the indigenous leaders. A number of ancient Celtic foundations adopted the Augustinian Order in the thirteenth century, including Bardsey, Beddgelert, and Penmon.

Gerald of Wales
Into this scene came one of Wales's most colourful personalities. Gerald de Barri, known as Gerald of Wales or Gireldus Cambrensis in Latin, was born in about 1146 in Manorbier, Pembrokeshire, and died in obscurity, possibly in Lincoln, in 1223. He was three parts Norman, one part Welsh, and typified in the body of one person the state of the Welsh nation at the time. On the one hand, he was blood-related to many Welsh leaders and was a relentless campaigner for a Church in Wales free from the jurisdiction of the Archbishop of Canterbury, with himself as its Archbishop of St Davids. On the other, he was well known to Henry II and many other establishment figures personally, accompanying Archbishop Baldwin around Wales and Herefordshire in 1188 to recruit for the Third Crusade. He held a number of establishment posts including the Archdeaconry of Brecon and a canonry of St Davids. Educated at Gloucester Abbey, he was groomed for a life in the church. His uncle David FitzGerald had been appointed Bishop of St Davids in 1148, and when he died in 1176 Gerald fought vigorously to obtain the post. His learning, integrity and reforming zeal were well-known to the king, but so also was his campaign for an independent Welsh church. Henry's memories of Thomas Becket who had troubled him so much only six years earlier, and the episode's tragic conclusion, were evidently still fresh in the king's mind, and so the dangerously independent-minded Gerald was passed over in favour of Peter de Leiâ, prior of the Cluniac house at Much Wenlock in Shropshire. Gerald therefore took himself off to Paris to study canon law and theology for the best part of a year, but when

he returned in 1176 he found de Leiâ at loggerheads with his chapter and having to live in England. The Archbishop of Canterbury gave Gerald administrative powers over the cathedral and he must have thought that this was his chance of landing the see, but relations with de Leiâ were repaired and he returned.

Peter de Leiâ began the rebuilding of St Davids Cathedral in 1181, and the quality of the nave, the first section to be rebuilt, shows that de Leiâ too was keen to demonstrate the pre-eminence of his see.

Meanwhile, Gerald accompanied Prince John to Ireland in 1185. He stayed there for a year, refusing the bishoprics of Wexford and then Leighlin, and then of both combined! In the 1190s bishop de Leiâ's health was failing, and Gerald refused bishoprics of both Bangor and Llandaff as he still had hopes of succeeding him. De Leiâ died in 1198 and there followed a five year battle for the see, during which Gerald spent much of this time in Rome pressing his case, but eventually the post went to Geoffrey de Henelawe, prior of Llanthony, in 1203. By now nearly sixty, Gerald abruptly withdrew from the fray, resigning his archdeaconry of Brecon and the prebend of Mathry.

He lived quietly for the last twenty years of his life, and it was during this period that he wrote the majority of his seventeen books. One of his earliest and best known however, researched in 1188 when he accompanied Archbishop Baldwin during his recruitment drive for the Third Crusade, was *Journey through Wales*. It is a valuable contemporary record of the state of the country at the time, and contains numerous wry and perceptive comments about the people he met and knew. Comments about buildings are frustratingly few; for instance Gerald makes no mention at all of the new nave of St Davids which was being built when he stayed there with Baldwin. However at Llanthony, thirteen years after building work had begun, he says it was 'roofed in with sheets of lead and built of squared stones which are admirably suited to the nature of the place.' He contrasts Llanthony with Llanthony Secunda, the house which had been established at Gloucester during the reign of King Stephen when the canons withdrew from Llanthony for their own safety, and says 'There in Gloucester men strive for earthly possessions, but here in Llanthony let them rather turn their minds towards the promise of eternal bliss.' Despite his inferences about the Gloucester house, he had more respect for the Augustinian Order than for the others, believing that they had adhered to their original ideals rather more closely, and had harsh words both for the worldly Benedictines and the avaricious Cistercians.

The Thirteenth Century
The early thirteenth century saw widespread building activity in Wales, and substantial Early English work can be seen for instance at St Davids, Brecon, Margam, AbbeyCwmhir (Llanidloes), Llandaff, Tintern, Neath, Beddgelert, Valle Crucis, and in a number of the parish churches. It indicated both the prosperity and, for the time being, the political stability which Wales enjoyed during this period. But it wasn't to last.

Montgomery castle, begun in 1223 by the sixteen-year-old Henry III, reflected the fact that the Welsh princes were re-asserting their authority and territorial claims throughout Wales, particularly in northern and central regions. By the mid-thirteenth century Llywelyn ap Gruffydd (Llywelyn the Last) was calling himself Prince of Wales. Henry III had plenty of trouble on his plate at home. The baronial revolt, led by Simon de Montfort, was by the mid-thirteenth century making great claims on the king's resources, and Henry had also been giving huge sums of money to the church. He had begun re-building Westminster Abbey in a lavish French style in 1245 as a counterpart to the coronation and royal burial church of Rheims in France, and he had also founded other abbeys. When de Montfort was defeated and killed in 1265 Henry was in neither the mood nor the financial position to embark upon campaigns in Wales, and so in 1267 he met Llywelyn at Montgomery and granted him the title of Prince of Wales, in return for the payment of a tribute of 25,000 marks. Llywelyn by this time was controlling much of north and central Wales, and if the Welsh had shown an inclination to unite behind such a strong leader, Wales might well have exploited the weaknesses of the English crown and pressed for its independence. But old rivalries between the princes prevented this, and in 1274 there was even a serious plot by Llywelyn's own brother, Dafyn, and another powerful Welch prince, Gruffydd ap Gwenwynwyn, to kill him.

Henry III had been an unpopular king, but he was a keen patron of the arts. His Westminster Abbey, built in a new and lavish style which was to become known as Decorated drew strong influences from France, and in its turn was to exert an equally strong influence upon the architecture of Britain, giving it a fresh impetus. Tintern Abbey's church was an obvious recipient of the new ideas, and Llandaff's Lady Chapel with its very tall side windows is again influenced by Westminster's clerestory. The geometric bar tracery characteristic of these buildings was adopted widely throughout Britain.

Henry died in 1272, and in 1274 his son Edward returned from the crusades to take the throne. Edward I already had experiences of war. He had played a large part in the defeat of de Montfort, and was a well-known and respected figure in Europe. A rather different animal from his father, Edward resolved to deal with the Welsh princes in a comprehensive manner. He cut off the funding for the rebuilding of Westminster Abbey leaving the nave still only half built, and marshalled all his resources for a serious campaign against the Welsh. It was to take three major campaigns between 1276 and 1295 before Edward could tour a demoralized Wales as its conqueror, but the fact that Beaumaris castle, the last of the great Edwardian fortresses in north Wales to be built, never had to be completed is an indication of how secure his position was by the end of the thirteenth century.

Edward's patronage of the church was nothing like as enthusiastic as his father's. His reign was to be one of military campaigns, and after the defeat of Wales he turned his attentions towards Scotland. He probably founded the friary at Carmarthen, and in 1270 before he became king he founded the Cistercian abbey of Vale Royal in Cheshire, a building planned on a lavish scale which may have been inspired by his father's Westminster Abbey, but funding had to be drastically curtailed during the years that followed and the original grand design was to be abandoned. In Wales, a number of the abbeys were caught up in the troubled years of the late thirteenth century, their allegiances either to the Welsh princes or to the crown inevitably placing them in a difficult position. Basingwerk, unusually an English-controlled Cistercian house in north Wales because of its close proximity to the Norman stronghold at Chester, was paid £100 in war damages by Edward. He also funded the rebuilding of Aberconway on a new site. Other houses which are known to have suffered serious damaged include Beddgelert, Grace Dieu, Neath, and Strata Florida. The latter, after suffering in the conflict in 1282, suffered a lightning strike in 1285 which caused even more damage. Whitland had been raided and robbed by Anglo-Normans in 1257 when Llywelyn was taking control of north Wales, and Edward paid the house no compensation for its losses during his wars because of its staunch support of Llywelyn. Valle Crucis was of course also a staunch supporter of the Welsh cause, but Edward was to pay £160 to the house for war damages. Cymer, another Welsh foundation, was visited by Edward on a number of occasions, and its abbot was obviously attempting to tread very carefully, for it received £80 from Edward in war damages. Generally though, damage to the religious houses was relatively minor compared to what was to happen early in the fifteenth century.

The Fourteenth Century
The first half of the fourteenth century was, for Wales, generally a period of calm, despite the fact that in the wake of Edward I's victory there was an influx of English settlers who populated the new borough towns, encircled within city walls, which were being established in the near vicinity of the castles. From these, the English were to dominate all aspects of Welsh government. During the first decades of the fourteenth century a good deal of building work was carried out throughout the religious houses. Edward II came to the throne in 1307, and though he was to prove one of England's least effective monarchs, his reign coincided with a great flowering of Decorated architecture, Britain taking the lead in Europe and exerting an influence upon France during the first quarter of the fourteenth century. Perhaps the lack of strong central patronage from the king encouraged the very diversity of styles, all however clearly recognisable as being of the period, which one sees at Llandaff, Brecon, St Davids, Valle Crucis, St Asaph, and Kidwelly. Establishment figures were appointed to the sees, and at St Davids, for instance, a succession of bishops included Thomas Bek (1280-93), chancellor of Oxford University; David Martin (1293-1327) and Henry de Gower (1328-47), also chancellors of Oxford; John Thoresby (1347-49), lord chancellor of England; and Adam de Houghton (1362-89), lord treasurer of England. St Davids was the largest and richest of the four sees of Wales, and those appointed as its bishops reflected its standing. The idea of a separate Church in Wales was for the time being a dead issue, although a number of the bishops appointed during this period were Welsh born, and were genuinely interested in Welsh affairs.

Edward III's reign was very different from that of his father. He came to the throne in 1327, and after successful campaigns in Scotland in the 1330s he and his son Edward the Black Prince spent much of their time campaigning in France. The king gave his son jurisdiction over much of Wales and three of its four sees, but he reserved control over St Davids, the largest and richest of them, for himself. During the second half of the century the king was taking a much closer interest in the election of bishops. Previously they had been chosen largely by the canons with papal approval, the king generally having little influence, but Edward III and his son were now appointing bishops and higher ranking clergy who would be useful to them politically, and many of those appointed were to have no previous connections with Wales. This enabled the king to take firmer economic control of the Principality, and taxes of various kinds were levied to fund his campaigns in France. Wales was to be seen as a source of revenue, and neither the king nor the Black Prince showed much interest in the spiritual wellbeing of the country. The economic prosperity of Wales, already showing signs of decline, was hit further in 1349 by the visitation of the Black Death, and afterwards it became increasingly difficult to recruit monks. The poll tax returns of 1377-81 illustrate the depleted numbers of monks then present in the monasteries: Llanthony had thirteen, Cwmhir had eight, Whitland had seven, and Carmarthen, Conwy and Talley each had just six. By comparison, Margam had 38 in 1326. The increasing strains on the financial resources of the religious houses as well as on their general decline is indicated by a report of 1368 which stated that Brecon Priory was in a ruinous state and in danger of closing. By 1380 Margam and Neath were seriously in arrears with their payments of tithes. Talley and St Dogmael's were in precarious financial positions. In the north, Conwy was deeply in debt to Italian merchants, and these debts had been accumulating since the mid fourteenth century. Beddgelert, Monmouth and Llantarnam all had to seek papal indulgences for their almost complete failure to function as monasteries at all. The Cistercians had originally eschewed the appropriation of parish churches as a source of revenue, but were now having to do so. Margam for instance succeeded in appropriating St Fagan's, Afon and Pen-llin, and by the dissolution it was found to be drawing 20% of its income from appropriations. The secular clergy were no better off, and the cathedrals were having to seek economic concessions.

The undoubted military prowess of Edward III and his son was sadly unmatched by that other essential weapon of any conflict, diplomacy, and during their brutal military successes they did nothing to win hearts and minds. The result for Wales and England was that she became artistically insular. Early in the century she had indeed influenced France, but now she was to develop a style of architecture, since known as Perpendicular, that was peculiar to Britain. It developed and flourished in England during the second half of the fourteenth century, but in Wales it tended to be confined to the abundant examples of Perpendicular window tracery, tomb designs and other relatively small scale works which can be seen in the parish and abbey churches, for there were no large building projects on anything like the scale of what was going on in England until late in the medieval period at parish church level.

The impoverished state of church and lay-society in Wales in the late fourteenth century fermented a level of unrest that was to be taken advantage of in full measure during the first decade of the following century.

Owain Glyndŵr

Owain Glyndŵr (*c*.1355-*c*.1415) was not quite the rebel that has sometimes been suggested. He was probably the richest man in Wales, a patron of the arts, lawyer, poet, and a soldier with a long record of loyal service to the English crown. Four of his five daughters were married to English landowners. He owned substantial estates, and in the late fourteenth century when Richard II was still on the throne he was evidently fairly happy with the *status quo*. His privileged status was cushioning him from the hardships that his fellow countrymen were suffering, and although he was quite aware of this, it took some provocative acts to stir him into action. Even when Henry Bolingbroke usurped Richard in 1399 to take the crown as Henry IV, Owain felt no particular inclination to revolt.

Lord Grey of Ruthin, a friend of Henry who had designs for acquiring additional lands in order to give him estates and a status comparable with those of the rather more anciently landed Marcher Lords, seized some of Owain's lands at Craesau between Ruthin and Glyndyfrdwy, an area that had long belonged to Owain's ancestors. Owain put his grievances before the king's parliament in 1399, and John Trevor, a Welsh landowner and bishop of St Asaph, counselled parliament to consider his good case carefully for fear of further unwelcome developments, but his advice was summarily ignored and the case was thrown out. Additionally, a writ for military services served by the king on Owain for his forthcoming campaigns against the Scots was not answered because it was deliberately held up by Grey in order to discredit him. Grey persuaded the king to send him to arrest Glyndŵr, and he evidently had his eyes on the rest of Owain's estates, but Owain was forced to take matters into his own hands. He took back what was rightfully his by force, to which act the king reacted by passing punitive laws forbidding any Welshman from holding a whole host of governmental and other official offices, whilst any posts held by them were to be immediately relinquished in favour of Englishmen. Additional taxes were also to be levied on the Welsh. Such inept and unworkable rulings might have been designed to fan the flames of rebellion, and so Owain Glyndŵr, a reluctant rebel who was quite evidently incensed at such provocative developments, declared himself Prince of Wales in 1400. Bishop Trevor's cathedral and palace were burned down by Glyndŵr's men during the early years of the conflict, but he joined the cause of the rebels in 1404.

There began more than a decade of strife which brought a great deal of destruction to religious houses as well as to many towns, all the more tragic because its cause had been so unnecessarily provoked by a new and headstrong king. But during the middle years of the first decade of that century, when Owain was controlling and consolidating much of Wales and the Marches, he set up court at Harlech castle and for a time had the breathing space to organize his government, sign a treaty with King Charles VI of France who too was at war with the English, make plans for an autonomous church of Wales with its own archbishop, and plan the founding of two universities, one in north Wales, one in the south.

Henry, suffering poor health throughout his reign which led to an early death at the age of 46 in 1413, was nevertheless a formidable adversary. He had to contend with war with the Welsh, wars with Scotland and France, unrest in Ireland, and political intrigues against him at home, but he survived all this, and when he was able to turn his attentions mainly towards the Welsh campaign, he and his able son, the future Henry V with whom he had entrusted the spearheading of the campaign, defeated Owain.

Among destruction visited upon the religious houses by both sides of the conflict, that at Strata Florida was particularly distasteful. Ystrad-fflur, Plain of Flowers, had been re-founded by The Lord Rhys in 1164 and was the burial place of eleven Welsh princes. Henry's army attacked the undefended abbey, killed many monks and took others prisoner, burnt and destroyed buildings, stole anything they could lay their hands on that was of any value, and stabled their horses at the high altar. Such accounts have much of the character of Oliver Cromwell's army's visits to the cathedrals during the English Civil War in the seventeenth century. For Glyndŵr's part, his army raised Abergavenny,

Usk, Caerleon, Newport and Cardiff early in the campaign, burning and looting wherever they encountered opposition to their cause. Monasteries such as Abergavenny, an alien priory which supported the king, can hardly have escaped considerable destruction, and the pattern was to be repeated throughout much of Wales.

After the Glyndŵr revolt, a state of near-lawlessness prevailed in large parts of Wales, and there were vendettas and reprisals among its people. Henry V's untimely death in 1422 left a weak and divided protectorate to govern England (Henry VI was only nine months old when his father died) and the onset of England's Wars of the Roses deprived the country of strong, purposeful government which would have benefited Wales during the difficult years after Glyndŵr. But the second half of the fifteenth century saw general improvements of the fortunes of the religious houses in Wales, albeit with somewhat reduced numbers of monks compared with former centuries. Appointments to the Welsh sees and upper clergy were still going largely to Englishmen. For instance Thomas Langton, a graduate of both Oxford and Cambridge and a chaplain to Edward IV and his ambassador to France, became bishop of St Davids in 1483, but by 1485 he had been translated to Salisbury. This was typical of the time.

The Tudor Era

When Henry Tudor defeated Richard III in battle to take the throne as Henry VII, however, the situation in Wales improved. He was born in Pembroke castle and had impeccable Welsh ancestry, but had visited England perhaps once before Bosworth, having spent many of his formative years in exile in France during England's turbulent warring. But he became king of England, and this astute, capable and, when needed, ruthless politician employed many Englishmen of distinction to provide a couple of decades a strong, stable administration. He did not neglect his countrymen, however, and in due course gave bishoprics to prominent Welshmen who had supported him during the years before he became king and during his office. But he had to recognise that Wales was a political backwater, and men of distinction could not always be spared in the Welsh dioceses for too long.

John Morgan became bishop of St Davids in 1496. An ardent Lancastrian, he had been active in the cause long before 1485. At St Asaph, two Welsh abbots succeeded each other. Dafydd ab Ieuan ab Iorwerth, abbot of Valle Crucis, became bishop there in 1500. He was a skilful politician and administrator, and had long supported Henry Tudor. Dafydd ab Owain succeeded him in 1503. An Oxford graduate and supporter of Henry, he had been successively abbot of Strata Florida, Strata Marcella and Conwy, doing much to revitalize the Cistercian Order in Wales as far as he was able to, and when he was made bishop he rebuilt the bishop's palace and took a conscientious interest in the see. A rejuvenation of the architecture of Wales and England had been gathering pace since the comparatively stable reign of Edward IV, and it flowered during Henry's reign, showing both the exuberance and something of the stylistic characteristics of the late Decorated period of two hundred years before. Henry's own chapel at Westminster Abbey where he is buried, an extraordinary building, pushed the style about as far as it could go.

Henry had christened his first born Arthur, and he was proclaimed Prince of Wales at the age of three. He died in Ludlow castle at the age of fifteen in 1502, and nothing significant has come down to us regarding his personality or what he might have become. We know rather more about his younger brother who was to take both Arthur's wife and the crown he would have worn, and his reign precipitated the dissolution of the monasteries. It also ushered in the Reformation. Henry VIII throughout his reign gave little more than lip-service to his Welsh ancestry, and the appointments to the higher clergy were once again being chosen largely from royal servants who were useful to him. It was to contribute greatly to the ease with which the monasteries could be closed, and the depleted numbers of incumbents in the religious houses by 1536 was in any case sending its own message to the abbots and priors about the continuing viability of monasticism. The Benedictine houses in the south, the earliest founded which were supported by the richer foreign patrons, had become the most impoverished. Brecon now had six monks, but Chepstow only had two, Ewenny three, and Monmouth two, these numbers being typical at the time. Cistercian houses generally had higher numbers of monks, but most were still in single figures: Valle Crucis had seven, Neath eight, and Whitland five. Tintern, always an 'English' house throughout its life, was unusual in having thirteen. The picture was very similar for the other Orders too.

The New World had been discovered, the world was suddenly a lot larger and more diverse than had previously been suspected, and the whole outlook of society was undergoing a change which was to leave the medieval world behind. Bibles were being manufactured on printing presses in England from the 1530s, and the role of monk as scribe and illuminator of manuscripts was also about to be eclipsed.

3

The Monastic Orders

The Benedictines take their name from St Benedict, an Italian saint canonized in 1220 who in 529 founded a monastery at Monte Casino in Italy. He compiled a set of regulations which became the basis of all later medieval monasticism. Towards the end of the sixth century the Order received the backing of Pope Gregory the Great, and there began the great Catholic religious movement with the Pope as its head which was to dominate Europe for almost a thousand years. Gregory was responsible for introducing Roman monasticism to England through his envoy St Augustine, and the latter's meeting with the Welsh, and his reception, has been mentioned in chapter 1. Augustine became the first Archbishop of Canterbury, and for the next hundred years monasticism spread throughout much of England. But it was almost completely destroyed in the eighth century by Danish invasions, and only Canterbury itself, and the Celtic monasteries in Wales and in the English West Country, survived. The monastic revival came in the tenth century with a general reform of the church in England led by Dunstan, Archbishop of Canterbury, Archbishop Oswald of York, and Bishop Ethelwold of Winchester. In about 970 the English bishops, abbots and abbesses met with King Edgar in Winchester where they drew up the Regularis Concordia. The old Benedictine Rule had been too vague, allowing a variety of regional customs and practices to exist and develop, and so the Regularis Concordia was

St Benedict of Nursia by Fra Angelico

St Augustine of Canterbury as depicted in the eighth-century Saint Petersburg Bede

St Dunstan (possibly a self-portrait) from the tenth-century Glastonbury Classbook

invoked to bring the monasteries under a strict, homogeneous regime. The ideals contained within it emphasised the observance of the liturgy, and intercessions for the living and the dead. There was also the requirement of the teaching of oblates: children given by their parents to become monks or nuns. Writing and illuminating of books, crafts and other chores within the monastery were also required, and a striving for the monastic ideal through chastity, obedience, austere living and an observance of the Rule of St Benedict were the ideals leading to salvation. The monks and nuns were to see themselves as the intermediary links between lay-society and God. These ideas had come from the Continent which had already seen recent reforms, and in England additional practices such as the attending of Sunday Mass by lay people in the abbey church, street processions by monks and nuns at festive times, and the choosing of a bishop from among the monks if the monastery served a cathedral, were also incorporated. But the history of monasticism after the Norman Conquest contains repeated attempts by new Orders to return to the original ideals which had gradually fallen by the wayside as a monastery became more affluent, politically entangled, and worldly in other ways.

The Benedictine monastery was usually ruled over by an abbot, and was therefore termed an abbey. The prior was his deputy. The Benedictine nunnery at Usk was ruled over by a prioress. If the church was also a cathedral as was the case with Canterbury, Ely, and Norwich for example, then the position of abbot was replaced by that of bishop. The prior was then effectively the head of the monastery, which was therefore termed a priory. There were no Welsh examples of this. Daughter houses or 'cells' were then sometimes established by these 'mother' houses. The abbot of the mother house was in principle also the head of the daughter house, with the prior of the daughter house (or priory) in effective control. Brecon Priory was founded in about 1100, a cell of Battle Abbey in Sussex. Those whose mother house was overseas, usually in France and frequently in Normandy, became known as alien priories, and in the immediate aftermath of the conquest of south Wales numerous such priories were established. Goldcliff Priory was affiliated to Bec in Normandy, Monmouth to St Florent in Saumur, and Pembroke to St Martin at Sées. A percentage of their income was creamed off by the mother houses, and this outflow of cash and goods to France later came to be resented by the English monarchs when the wars with both France and Scotland in the fourteenth and fifteenth centuries were bringing England to the brink of bankruptcy. Additional taxes were already levied on the alien priories, but during the fifteenth century a handful of the smaller houses were dissolved and the monks dispersed to other monasteries. The rest were compelled to sever their overseas ties.

The Cluniac Order, taking its name from its first foundation at Cluny in Burgundy in 910, founded just two small cells in Wales (Malpas and St Clears). Their overriding concern was the liturgy, with an emphasis on elaborate ceremonies, daily psalms and prayers, the singing of the Office, and the giving of alms by the monks to the poor. Less emphasis was placed upon teaching, intellectual pursuits, and the writing and illumination of books, and the Order received praise for its high religious ideals and its lack of involvement with political affairs. A total of 36 Cluniac priories were established in England (all Cluniac houses were priories, daughter houses of Cluny) but only Lewes in Sussex achieved a stature comparable with the great Benedictine houses.

St Bernard of Clairvaux, from a medieval illuminated script

The Cistercian Order was founded in 1098 at Cîteaux (Latin: *Cistercium*) in Burgundy, and was soon joined by St Bernard of Clairvaux who did much to promote its development. It was born out of a desire to return to the original Benedictine ideal which had become somewhat diluted. The Cistercians were known as the White Monks because they wore un-dyed habits, in contrast to the Benedictine Black Monks. Emphasis was on a strict adherence to the Benedictine Rule, and their houses were deliberately established in remote areas. They sometimes even removed existing settlements from their chosen sites in striving for their ideals, whereas towns grew up around the Benedictine houses generating much contact between the monks and the townspeople. The austere Cistercian ideals were, in the early decades at least, reflected in their architecture, their houses being characterized by a formalized ground plan with none of the lavish carving in the stone which was to adorn later Cistercian building work at Valle Crucis and Margam for example. The elaborate Norman-style carving which one sees at Penmon would have been unthinkable in the contemporary nave of Margam Abbey. There were no Lady Chapels, elaborate chapter houses, or high central towers. All the houses were ruled over by an abbot, and were thus termed abbeys. The abbots, or their representatives, travelled to Cîteaux each year for an annual general Chapter, and in this way the original ideals could in theory be preserved.

In contrast to the Benedictines, the Cistercians renounced all wealth, refusing to accept gifts of manors which were already populous and flourishing. They exercised no monopoly over mills, fishing rights, or the administration of law, and they generally remained aloof from the society which they had left behind. There were no special masses or prayers offered for patrons, no chantry chapels, and no cults built around saints or relics which could be an important source of revenue for the Benedictine houses. Their churches were always dedicated to the Virgin Mary, or occasionally there was a joint dedication. In contrast to the Cluniacs, there were no elaborate processions, litanies or psalms, little chanting, and no special services for saints' days. Their three main ideals were the preserving of the Opus Dei in its purest form, hard work, and the study of the scriptures and private prayer. There was no teaching of oblates, and sixteen was the minimum age at which a novice would be admitted. A year's exacting instruction would be given before a novice became a regular monk. The Order of Savigny had very similar ideals. Founded soon after 1100 by a canon of the Collegiate church of St Evroul called Vitalis of Mortain, he established a hermitage in the forest of Savigny in France, resigning his prebend to lead a more contemplative and unworldly life. But by the mid twelfth century the Order had been absorbed by the Cistercians.

Cistercian houses were established throughout Wales, those in the south such as Tintern (founded in 1131, one of the earliest in Britain) and Margam generally being founded by the Anglo-Norman conquerors. Those to the north and west were generally founded by the Welsh rulers who had recognised the value of patronizing the church, but Basingwerk in the far north, originally a Savignac house, was a Norman foundation. Two Cistercian nunneries were also founded, at Llanllugan and Llansantffraed in Elfael, both in Powys. As the twelfth century progressed, the Cistercian ideal gradually began to subside, and by the time of the dissolution there was no clear distinction between Benedictine and Cistercian houses apart from the remote locations of the latter. One can contrast the elaborate architecture of Margam's east end and chapter house, which were being built from about 1200, with the very austere nave of only fifty years earlier.

The Augustinian Canons Regular, or Austin canons as they became known in Britain, established themselves in England soon after 1100. In Wales, William de Lacy took shelter in an old ruined chapel at Llanthony in the Black Mountains whilst on a hunting expedition, and there he decided to take up a life of religious contemplation. It became his hermitage. By the end of the first decade of the twelfth century his fame had drawn many followers, and by 1125 there were about forty Canons there living under the Augustinian Rule. A Canon was originally a clerk living according to a rule (from the Greek: *kanòn* – rule) and during the eleventh century there was a movement to bring the canons under a rather stricter, monastic way of living. Canons were often married, but there was a Papal campaign to adopt celibacy generally among the Catholic clergy as part of a wider move to free it from the regular social institutions of secular life.

The Lateran Council of 1059, whilst not actually enforcing monastic rule upon the Augustinians, nevertheless urged a monastic way of life embodying chastity, poverty, and the submission to a Rule and a prior. Over two hundred Augustinian houses were established in Britain by 1350, most of which were termed priories. Only thirteen achieved the status of an abbey. The Regular Canons who peopled them were distinct from the Secular Canons who followed the older, more worldly Orders, and who governed the secular (i.e. non-monastic) cathedrals.

A sixth-century depiction of St Augustine of Hippo

The Rule was based on a letter of St Augustine of Hippo in the fifth century which offered advice to North African houses which were being established at the time. It was augmented by sections contained in the Benedictine Rule, and the result was an Order less strict than the contemporary Cistercian and original Benedictine one. The daily Office was shorter, rules governing the taking of food and drink were less restrictive, more conversation was allowed, and there could be more freedom of movement among the lay-community. The Augustinian houses were characterized as much by their variety as by their similarity: some dominated towns, for instance at Cirencester. Some were more Cistercian-like, as at Llanthony and Bardsey. Carlisle became a cathedral soon after it was founded. A small number served hospitals, as did Penmon Priory on Anglesey. Some Austin canons served as priests in parish churches which were part of the priory's endowment. The Austin Canons were well regarded and patronized by lay-people and royalty, being a monastic Order which also interested itself in the secular community. Augustinian houses of Canonesses were also established, although none in Wales.

The Tironensian Order originated at Tiron in France, in 1109. Basically Benedictine, emphasis was on a simplified liturgy, an austere daily life, and on the practising of skilled crafts within the confines of the convent. The Order achieved a significant presence only in Scotland, but a Tironensian abbey was founded at St Dogmael's in Dyfed. Daughter priories were established on Caldey Island, and at Pill in Dyfed.

The Premonstratensian houses of Regular canons originated at Prémontré near Laon in France. In 1120, St Norbert, a wandering evangelical preacher, based his house on the Cistercian ideal, and from the mid twelfth century more than thirty such houses were established in Britain. But their close affinity with the already well-established Cistercian Order meant that they never flourished, the need for this type of Order already having been catered for. All Premonstratensian houses were abbeys, and one was established in Talley in Dyfed.

Other Orders played little or no part in the monastic landscape of Wales, so the following outline of two of them is very brief.

The Carthusian Order was a breakaway from the Cluniacs, taking its name from the French town of Chartreuse, where the first house was founded by St Bruno in the twelfth century. In these Charterhouses, as they were known, emphasis was on an even more simple and severe life than hitherto, each monk living in a cell with its own small garden in almost complete solitude. The cells were grouped around a cloister, and a communal church was visited much less frequently than was the case with the other Orders. There is some resemblance to the Celtic monastery in layout, if not in outlook. Only nine Carthusian houses were established in England, and they were all priories, daughter houses of Grand Chartreuse.

The Gilbertine Order was the only Order founded by a Briton. Gilbert of Sempringham, a twelfth-century Lincolnshire priest, established a convent for nuns under Benedictine Rule, and it was administered by Augustinian Canons. A total of twenty-six houses were founded, half of them in Gilbert's lifetime, all of them being priories of Regular Canons. The Canons and nuns had separate cloisters, but shared a church within which was a wall to separate the two communities. The houses were ruled jointly by a prior and a prioress.

The running of each convent of whatever Order required that jobs were allocated to obedientiaries, individuals responsible for overseeing the various activities and duties of the house. As has been noted, the prior was the deputy of the abbot, or in the case of a daughter house or a cathedral priory he was effectively in control. He was assisted by a sub-prior, and also sometimes by a third prior. The team of obedientiaries included the precentor, who was responsible for arranging the services in the church. The sacrist looked after the church furnishings such as the altar crosses, lecterns, plate, and other fittings. The cellarer looked after the convent's provisions. The almoner was responsible for giving alms to the poor by the gate; communities of poor and infirm people were often sustained by the larger houses in this way. The chamberlain was responsible for clothing and bedding. The infirmarer was in charge of the farmery (or infirmary). The porter was the keeper of the gate, and oversaw the traffic entering and leaving the precinct. The refectorer saw to the table linen and the lighting, and also obtained provisions for the cellarer.

The foundation and endowment of a convent, whether as an act of piety tinged with political expediency as was the case with the Normans, a shrewd move by a Welsh ruler, or a seemingly innocent bringing into being from humbler beginnings as at Llanthony, afterwards required an income for its maintenance, which in part could be met by an output of goods or services. The cathedrals and Benedictine houses particularly, in addition to the endowments from their founders, had sources of income connected with the celebrations of masses for departed members of aristocratic families. The chapels which one still sees in St Davids and in many cathedrals and greater abbeys brought with them endowments in return for which the monks or clergy would give special prayers. Parishes were often ceded to them, from which the convents received tithes and other endowments. In return, the convent would be responsible for the maintenance of the chancel of the parish church, the parish being responsible for the nave. Presteigne parish church in Powys is a good example of the latter arrangement, the chancel having been financed by the Augustinian Canons of nearby Wigmore. Sometimes, the nave of the abbey church itself would be used as the parish church as was usually the case with the Benedictines, and this frequently brought conflict between the monastic and lay communities. The priest was paid by the convent, and in earlier times it was a proverbially mean sum, although the Lateran Council of 1215 decreed that the parish priest should be given a decent living which included the use of a vicarage. The convents also became considerable landowners through various endowments and wills, and this was systematically put to profitable use. Large Benedictine houses and cathedrals obtained much revenue from pilgrims visiting their holy shrines. Canterbury had the tomb of St Thomas Becket who was murdered in his own church; Durham had the relics of St Cuthbert; St Albans Abbey had the shrine of St Alban; and St Peter's Abbey in Gloucester had managed to acquire the body of Edward II. Worcester had the tomb of King John. In Wales, St Davids Cathedral had the shrine of its founding saint, and its popularity was bolstered by David's canonization by Pope Callixtus II (d.1124) and his proclamation that two pilgrimages to St Davids were equal to one to Rome. In north Wales there was St Winifred's Well in Holywell where the Welsh-born Henry V came to give thanks after his victory at Agincourt, and today it still receives many visitors. St Beuno was responsible for bringing Celtic monasticism to much of north Wales, and he was said to have restored his niece Winifred to life after her head had been severed by a rejected lover. The well belonged to nearby Basingwerk Abbey until the dissolution. At Usk Priory, there was the Shrine of St Radegund, a German or Frankish noble-born woman who in the sixth century had taken the veil and founded an abbey at Poitiers.

The Cistercian, and a number of the Augustinian, houses were deliberately situated in the wilds, and many of the above sources of income were unavailable to them. They therefore placed a heavy emphasis on farming, and wool became a major source of income. Fishing was also an enthusiastic activity, and Valle Crucis's large fish pond can still be seen. The Taxatio Ecclesiastica of 1291 records that Margam Abbey had 5,285 sheep, Neath 4,879, Basingwerk 2,000, and Tintern, 3,264.

Tintern's wool was especially prized, and it fetched a good price. The Cistercians generally acquired a reputation for avarice, and their zeal had obviously stemmed from the need to turn their remote foundations into viable going concerns. There was a flourishing wool export trade, for instance, and it was not only the Cistercians who were involved in the production of wool.

A network of monastic granges were set up, each ideally being no more than a single day's journey from the abbey, from which the convent's employees could attend to the farming. Lay-brothers, or *conversi*, played an important part in the economy of Cistercian houses, and they lived in the monastery in separate quarters from the monks under a less strict rule. The nave of the church was used by them for worship since they were not themselves monks, and the choir was reserved for the Cistercian monks' worship.

The Friars

The friars were not strictly monks at all, founding their houses in centres of population in order to pursue an evangelizing campaign. The layout of their establishments varied but resembled that of the monastic Orders in a number of ways, and parts of their churches have survived at Brecon and Denbigh. The friars were strictly mendicants, initially living by charity almost on a day to day basis, renouncing all wealth and worldly possessions to an extent even greater than the Cistercian ideal.

The older monastic Orders could claim credit for the spiritual and educational advances which society had seen generally during the course of the twelfth century, but the growth of the population and its greater prosperity in the thirteenth had brought with it needs with respect to teaching and general spiritual and intellectual questionings which those Orders were ill-equipped to supply. It was the friars who largely answered these needs, although they were originally founded for a slightly different purpose.

In Europe towards the end of the twelfth century there was a growth of a movement which questioned the established articles of faith, seeking to replace them with new truths. Heresies were preached, and the movement began to spread. This Catharist or Albigensian heresy originated in the Balkans, and it began to attract Christians in northern Italy, the Rhineland, southern France and the Low Countries, but it scarcely appeared at all in Britain. The Popes were naturally worried about this development as Catharism, which claimed to be Christian, was really an alternative faith. The Cathars observed that the world was by and large an evil place, and that therefore it must have been created by the devil, rather than by God, and that it was God who had come into the domain of the devil to do good. The friars owed their origin to this heresy, as they were created to give support to the bishops and clergy in their fight against the new belief, acting as itinerant preachers of the true faith. It is ironic that they were subsequently perceived to be a threat to the established monastic Orders and particularly to the parish clergy.

Dominic of Osma (1170-1221) was an Augustinian canon in Spain, founding his order of Dominican or black friars along the lines of personal poverty, dedicated to an

*St Dominic of Osma
by Giovanni Bellini*

intellectual campaign against the Catharist heresy. His friars were well schooled, intellectually alert, and equipped to carry the message to the general population with a new verve which the regular clergy were less ready to do. There was less emphasis on a daily Office, much study of logic and theology, and a campaign of preaching both in the pulpit and in writing. The movement was therefore in some ways an adaptation of monasticism to an evangelizing crusade among the population in the towns.

St Francis of Assisi (1181-1224) was a rich, noble-born Italian layman, called to follow the paths of humility and poverty, and he aspired to follow Jesus in the way he lived. He gave himself up to a life of prayer and total poverty, living only on the alms of others, and dedicated himself to helping the sick and the needy, especially the lepers, whilst also preaching his message. He shunned all intellectual pursuits together with money, property, and also protection from the law. Wishing to found no Order, he nevertheless attracted many followers, and when he died having adhered to all of his strict ideals, it was his followers who founded the Franciscan order of grey friars. Unlike Dominic, Francis had provoked conflict within the church itself. The Franciscans preached, heard confessions, absolved sinners, and administered mass, and this was an intrusion into the work of the bishops and their clergy. In the fourteenth century St Francis' literal adherence to his ideal of poverty

St Francis of Assisi by El Greco

was itself actually made a heresy, part of a more general campaign against the Lollards, followers of the reformer John Wycliffe, who taught that pious layman should have the power to perform the same rites as the established clergy. There was a growing belief that religious power and authority came through piety and not through the Church hierarchy, and Thomas Arundel, Archbishop of Canterbury, was one of the leaders in the campaign against the movement. It had no significant impact in Wales, and had the characteristics of a nonconformist movement that had emerged a couple of hundred years before its time.

There was rivalry between the Dominican and Franciscan Orders. The Dominicans' ideal had not originally included the strict poverty of the Franciscans, but they soon took it up. The Franciscan shunning of learning was soon abandoned as they strove to be as learned as their rivals, an essential goal if their missions against heresy were to be successful. In fact a number of outstanding intellectual figures of the thirteenth century, including Roger Bacon, were Franciscan friars. The enthusiastic sermons of the friars soon attracted large congregations, and people began to take confession with them and be buried in their graveyards. The bishops soon began to restrict their activities as they were becoming too successful for comfort; for instance they licensed only a rigidly limited number of friars to take confessions.

The friars were generally welcomed in Britain despite conflicts with the established church, the bishops being well informed about developments on the Continent. They were given lectureships, donations and sites for their convents, and Henry III, an enthusiastic patron of the church, was especially generous to them, using them as confessors. Friars were also often sent on diplomatic missions abroad, and it was the Franciscans particularly who contributed much to European philosophy.

By the mid-thirteenth century other lesser orders of friars had been formed. The Austin friars (distinct from the Austin or Augustinian canons) were closely modelled on the Dominicans. The Carmelites, or white friars, were basically Dominican but were the most contemplative Order among the friars. They were closer to monks in general outlook, and even founded a small number of houses away from the towns. The remains of the Carmelite friary church at Denbigh are a mile to the east of the town. There were also Friars of the Holy Cross or Crutched Friars, and Friars of the Penitential Sack or Pied Friars. These were all basically Dominican, the Franciscans becoming the minority whilst still remaining vigorous. St Francis had had women followers, and St Clare had professed her vows before St Francis himself. She founded a second Order of Franciscans, but the other Orders remained exclusively male.

The older monastic Orders had considerably increased their wealth throughout the twelfth and thirteenth centuries, and there grew a certain amount of resentment among the lay community who had formerly patronized them. The friars achieved their popularity partly as a result of their renunciation of all wealth and possessions; the Franciscans for instance went bare-foot even in winter. But by the end of the thirteenth century even the friars had become more worldly with their endowments, extensive convents, and small-holdings. Their assets were in fact held in trust because both of the movement's founders had forbidden the possession of property and money, but this had become something of a technicality.

Later developments

The number of convents of all kinds had steadily increased throughout the twelfth and thirteenth centuries, and by the end of the thirteenth the building pattern had become one of extension and rebuilding in the latest style. In England the motivation was often the desire of an abbot, bishop or patron to leave his mark on the fabric, and to keep the house in the vanguard of fashion. This was also the case in Wales, but in many instances rebuilding had become necessary after wanton destruction during conflicts with the Anglo-Normans in the twelfth century, Edward I in the thirteenth, various Welsh uprisings, and Owain Glyndŵr's rebellion after 1400.

The Black Death of 1349 and in subsequent years had a devastating effect on Europe, and it has been estimated that about one third of Britain's population perished. This hastened the movement away from the feudal system with its economy based on land, worked by serfs, which was held by vassals in exchange for military and other services to overlords, towards an economy based on wages. The shortage of workers in the immediate aftermath of the Black Death had an effect on the Cistercian Order particularly, and from this time it became increasingly difficult to recruit lay-brothers. The development of the waged economy had drawn them away and the lay-brother ceased to play a significant role in the organization of the Cistercian house.

By the end of the fifteenth century there were about eight hundred religious houses in Wales and England. Building programmes had continued: many timber screens in Wales date from this time, and St Davids saw the building of its Holy Trinity Chapel, nave roof and upper stage of the tower. Newport and Llandaff had received impressive western towers, and Tintern had received a large new farmery. Bangor Cathedral had been largely rebuilt during the fifteenth and early sixteenth centuries following devastation at Owain Glyndŵr's hands. But money was now being diverted to the parish church rather than to the monasteries, and the latter were finding it increasingly difficult to recruit monks and nuns. Society was changing, and its consequences for the monastic establishments and the coming of the Reformation are covered elsewhere in this book.

4

Architecture: The Monastic Inheritance

The first requirement of architecture is that its buildings should be capable of performing their intended functions. The monastery was akin to a town in microcosm, and so within its confines there had to be provision for the worship of God, living quarters, eating quarters, sleeping quarters, a meeting house, kitchens, latrines, study areas, visitors' quarters, quarters for the old and the sick, storage space, a fresh water supply, and water drainage. The standardized plan which the Normans brought with them was a typical example of the efficiency and organizational skills which that culture had applied to its various campaigns throughout Europe, and it will be looked at in detail. The pre-Conquest Westminster Abbey which included many of its features was a reflection of considerable Norman influence decades before 1066 rather than of indigenous developments, notwithstanding its very long nave compared with the great majority of the churches which were built in Normandy during the tenth and eleventh centuries.

For the monastery to function efficiently, its buildings had to be planned and laid out in a logical manner, appropriate both for their individual tasks and for convenient movement among them. The cloister was therefore a large, covered walkway laid out to a square or rectangular plan to provide easy communication between the various buildings which would be grouped around it. The church, the largest building of the group, had to provide ample room for the choir, the high altar, walkways in the form of side and cross aisles for use in processions, chapels with their altars, and a nave. This necessarily dictated the construction of a large building which would also need to be tall in order to generate the necessary sense of scale and grandeur, a fitting building for the house of God. The other buildings, of more or less utilitarian function, could nevertheless display considerable artistic merit, as the various illustrations will show. It is an indication that the foundation was seen not just as a place to conduct the business of the convent, but also to express God's majesty as fully as possible in artistic terms, and the two went hand in hand in shaping the form and nature of the architecture which it brought into being.

Figure 1 shows a typical post-Conquest monastic plan. It is based upon no particular foundation because there were many variations of detail. The church was the largest and most important building, and was almost invariably orientated with the nave pointing in a westerly direction and the presbytery pointing eastward as shown. Except in Cistercian churches the nave (1) was sometimes used for worship by the lay community, occasionally parts of it being taken over and used as the parish church. Extensions for this purpose were sometimes built: at both Abergavenny and Usk north aisles were built onto the existing naves, and Leominster Priory in Herefordshire still has its enormous thirteenth- and fourteenth-century nave extensions to the south, reflecting the growing population and prosperity of the town through successive centuries. Cistercian houses were remotely sited; members of the lay community were not permitted to worship in the church, and so a chapel for layfolk was normally provided outside the precincts. The nave was used

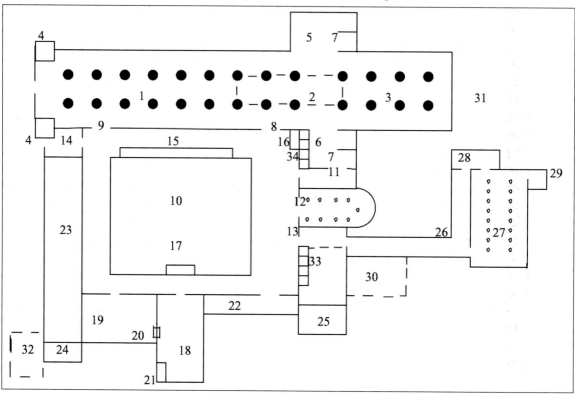

Fig. 1 Ground plan of a typical monastery complex

1. Nave	13. Eastern parlour	24. Lay-brothers' rere-dorter
2. Choir	14. Western parlour	25. Monks' reredorter
3. Presbytery	15. Scriptorium	26. Cloister of eastern range
4. Western towers	16. Book cupboard	27. Farmery (infirmary)
5. North transept	17. Lavatorium	28. Farmery (infirmary) kitchen
6. South transept	18. Monks' frater	29. Chapel
7. Chapels	19. Monks' kitchen	30. Abbot's lodgings
8. Eastern processional door	20. Serving hatch	31. Cemetery
9. Western processional door	21. Pulpit	32. Guest's lodgings
10. Cloister garth	22. Warming house	33. Monks' day stair
11. Sacristy or slype	23. The west range	34. Monks' night stair
12. Chapter house		

28

for worship by the considerable number of lay-brothers or *conversi* who lived within the cloister, and who performed the manual tasks and looked after the farming. The two side aisles of the nave shown in the plan, being divided from the central aisle by a series of arches called an arcade, played a part in the processions and afforded an opportunity for architectural display, but they were not always present. The compartment which each arch defines is called a bay, and so the nave on the plan is of nine bays.

The pair of western towers (4) would form part of an imposing west front as at Llanthony, but being liturgically of minimal use they were often omitted. Llanthony is the only monastic example in Wales.

The choir (2), sometimes spelt quire, is the area where the monks or canons performed their services. It was often situated beneath the central tower in the crossing space where the nave, transepts and presbytery meet as shown, and it also frequently extended west of the crossing to include two or more eastern bays of the nave. The monks would sit in rows of stalls facing each other to the north and south across the choir, and additional return stalls would be placed to the west of the choir facing eastwards.

The presbytery (3) to the east of the choir was a clear space for the use of processions and ceremonies, east of which was the sanctuary and High Altar. Behind the altar there would sometimes be an ambulatory around which processions could go, known as the retro-choir. This eastern arm is shown with north and south aisles, but they were often absent. It is in the eastern section of the church where the main differences with the parish church lie. The latter was usually divided into a nave and a chancel, the chancel being the domain of the clergy which incorporated the altar. Later a three-compartment plan was adopted consisting of nave, choir and chancel, but there was no provision for the rituals which were performed in the cathedrals and abbeys.

The apsidal eastern end, either in the form of a semi-circle as shown on the plan's chapter house (12) or in the form of a semi-polygon as at Llanthony, remained popular in France for the eastern chapels of the transepts and choir aisles, and also as a termination for the presbytery itself. But in Britain from the mid-twelfth century onwards it was abandoned in favour of the rectangular chapel and the square east end. The splendid apsidal ambulatories at Peterborough, Westminster, Norwich and Tewkesbury, the latter three with radiating chapels in the form of the French *chevet*, gradually became exceptions to the rule. But there certainly wasn't an aversion to the circular or polygonal form, and conversely the polygonal chapter houses which became so popular in Britain have no parallel in France.

Numbers 5 and 6 are the north and south transept arms respectively. They provide access to small eastern chapels (7) for the private celebration of mass. Four chapels are shown but there were often three to each transept. In the Benedictine houses and cathedrals, where endowments from rich patrons required the saying of special prayers for them, additional chapels and alters would be placed in the nave and at eastern ends of the choir aisles, and also in the transepts wherever there was room.

Chantry chapels, virtually separate chambers in their own right, were also built as a result of the endowments of bishops and other patrons, and Bishop Vaughan's Chapel, the Holy Trinity Chapel, behind the high altar at St Davids is a good example.

Number 8 is the eastern processional doorway leading out into the east walk of the cloister, and number 9 is the western processional doorway. The latter was traditionally

Fig. 2 Valle Crucis Abbey. This overview clearly shows the layout of the buildings as described in the text. The church is on the left to the north, with the cloister garth on the right around which was grouped the conventual buildings. In the background is the entrance to the chapter house, above which is built the monks' dormitory

Fig. 3 Penmon Priory, showing an alternative arrangement mainly as a result of adapting an existing church to monastic use. A house was built onto the south transept after the dissolution. In the centre is the early thirteenth-century south range, unusual in having three storeys. The frater was built over an undercroft, with the dorter above that. The eastward extension was built in the early sixteenth century to contain the kitchen and the warming house. On the right is a dovecot which was built in about 1600

absent in Cistercian houses, because Sunday processions which would take in the cloister walkways and chapter house would in these houses also take in the lay-brothers' quarters in the western range, re-entering the church by the west door shown between the two towers rather than by the western processional doorway. The west door would normally be covered by a canopy or porch, known as a narthex if this were the case. However, this was by no means universal in Cistercian houses, and at Basingwerk for instance there was a western doorway leading into the church from the cloister. The doorway north of centre in the west wall of the nave was a later addition. At Cymer, a west door is not present because an axial west tower was built in the fourteenth century after the plan to build the crossing over which a tower could be placed, together with an eastern arm for the church, had been cancelled.

Fig. 4 St Davids. The new cloisters, designed by Peter Bird, house meeting rooms and a treasury among the facilities

Number 10 is the cloister garth, an open, grassed space contained by the cloister walkways. Sometimes it was used by the monks for growing herbs to be used in medicines in the farmery. The cloisters, the four walkways forming the square around the garth, were an important part of the convent. They were conventionally sited to the south of the nave so that the church would give shelter from the cold north winds whilst allowing the sun to the south to give warmth. Expediencies of site, for example the provision of drainage, would sometimes mean that the cloister and other conventual buildings would have to be sited to the north as at Tintern, and the layout would then become a mirror image of that shown on the plan. Occasionally eccentricities of plan are encountered. Penmon Priory on Anglesey had a presbytery which was larger than the nave, and the cloisters were sited south of this eastern arm. This was due to the fact that the Augustinians came to Penmon nearly a century after the nave and original east end had been built, and a new presbytery was constructed for the canons with the conventual buildings sited south of it.

The inner wall of the cloister consisted of an arcade upon a low plinth, and the walkways would be roofed over and often vaulted in stone. This afforded another opportunity for architectural display, and very fine examples have survived at Canterbury, Gloucester, Norwich and Worcester for example. At the secular cathedrals where cloisters were not strictly necessary they were still often indulged in as a display of architectural splendour, and good examples can be seen at Salisbury, Lincoln and Wells. It is a great pity that none have survived in Wales, but the modern interpretation of the form at St Davids, designed to serve contemporary needs, is welcome.

Number 11 is the sacristy where vessels, garments, valuables, and sometimes books would be kept, whilst number 12 is the chapter house, second only in importance to the church itself. Here there would be a meeting when a chapter of the Rule would be read, discussions about the day's business held, and conduct of the monks examined. It was also often used as a burial place for abbots and benefactors of the abbey. The early Cistercian chapter houses were usually plain rectangular buildings with aisles, sometimes with an apsidal eastern end as shown on the plan, if arrangements above would permit. Elsewhere, and later even in Cistercian houses, the chapter house was to become another opportunity for architectural expression. Worcester has a rotund chapter house which dates probably from the first decade of the twelfth century, and recent archaeological excavations have revealed Saxon work in the foundations. It could be then that the apsidal termination of a pre-existing building was used as the basis for the chapter house, the curve being continued around to complete a circle to form the rotund building that we see today. Whatever its origins, Worcester's attractive room inspired no immediate imitators, and it was not until about 1200 that Margam Abbey began building a splendid twelve-sided chapter house with a central pier of clustered shafts developing into an elaborate vault fanning out from the centre. Around the periphery was arranged the seating. This set a fashion in Britain, and soon rotund chapter houses appeared at Lincoln, Westminster Abbey, Southwell, York, Beverley, Wells, Salisbury and many other places. The Cistercians also built polygonal chapter houses at Abbey Dore near Hereford, and at Whalley in Lancashire.

Number 13 is the eastern parlour (from the French *parler*, to speak) or slype, where talking was permitted. On this plan it also forms a walkway to the eastern range of buildings. This area at ground-floor level was sometimes taken up by novices' quarters. Number 14 is the western parlour where discussions could take place with the lay-brothers and with visitors with whom business was transacted.

At 15, the walkway of the cloister adjacent to the nave of the church, was the scriptorium. Here the monks would study, write and illuminate books. Sometimes there is evidence of a prior's seat towards the centre where he would overlook the proceedings. In Cistercian houses there would be an abbot's seat against the wall of the church mid way along the walk. The Collation, a reading before Compline, would be given by the abbot from here. At 16 there would often be a recess in the wall for a book cupboard.

Fig. 5 Basingwerk. The monks' frater. At the far end can just be seen a blocked doorway which gave access to a stairway leading up to the pulpit

Fig. 6 Tintern. The washing-up sink in the monks' frater

Such a recess can still be seen at Brecon Cathedral, which was formerly a Benedictine priory. Sometimes book cupboards would be situated adjacent to the chapter house as can be seen at Valle Crucis, and one can also encounter them in the west walk near the novices' quarters.

At 17 is the monks' lavatorium where they would wash before entering the frater. Nearby there would be recesses in the walls for towels.

Number 18 is the monks' frater or refectory. It could be a large elaborate building resembling a great hall, and it was also often built above a vaulted undercroft which was used to store ale, wine and other provisions. The orientation on the plan is north-south. Early Cistercian houses favoured an east-west orientation for the frater, as was also the case at Augustinian Llanthony where the scars of the undercroft's vaulting ribs can still be seen against the wall, but later Cistercian houses often adopted the orientation shown as it allowed more room for the monks' kitchen, 19, where meals were prepared. Number 20 is a serving hatch, and 21 is a raised pulpit from which a monk would read passages from the scriptures during meals.

Number 22 was the warming house. Apart from in here fires were allowed in only two other places, the kitchen and the farmery (27). The other buildings, including the church itself, were completely unheated, and the discomfort during the long services during the winter months can be appreciated. The climate here was rather less congenial to the monks than that prevailing somewhat further to the south-east where monasticism began and developed. If in dire need a monk could go to the warming house for a period of recovery.

Number 23 usually took the form of a vaulted undercroft or cellar for storage over which, in Cistercian houses, was built the lay-brothers' dorter (dormitory), frater and common room. To the north, over the western parlour, there would often be a night stair giving access to the nave of the church. Number 24 was their rere-dorter or latrine housing a row of cubicles with appropriately designed seats to discharge waste into the drainage system to the south. In other houses 23 could be used as guests' quarters, or for administration, or as a library.

The monks' dorter was often built over the sacristy, chapter house and eastern parlour, continuing southwards to their rere-dorter at 25. Sometimes it was situated just to the south of the chapter house if the latter was a tall structure precluding the building of accommodation above it. The dorter was a large communal space initially, but later it was often

Fig. 7 Valle Crucis. The monks' dorter. The doorway at the far end led to the night stairs

partitioned off using timber to form separate cubicles for the monks. Access during daylight hours was via the day stair at 33, and the night stair at 34 gave the monks access to the church via the south transept when they went to perform mass at around 2am. These stairs, usually of timber, are rarely to be seen today but one often sees the doorway leading from the dorter high up in the south wall of the south transept, often now blocked. Remains of the night stair can be seen at Neath, and Tintern has a reconstructed one. At Haverfordwest the night stair was built into the thickness of the west wall of the south transept, and at Ewenny there is a newel stair built into the corner of the transept.

Number 26 forms an eastern cloister leading to the eastern range of buildings. Number 27 is the farmery or infirmary where the sick would be attended to. This would sometimes be used as a hospital for lay people as well as for the inmates. It was normally aisled as shown, with the beds placed in the aisles. The central walkway was left clear, the layout resembling a hospital ward. Those inmates who had become too old or infirm to perform their duties would lodge here. It would also serve as a resting place for the monks after their blood-letting, a procedure to which the monks submitted to several times a year, as it was deemed to cleanse the soul and preserve good health. Number 28 was the kitchen serving the farmery, and the diet here was rather more liberal than that served in the other kitchens in view of the state of the incumbents. The farmery had its own chapel (29).

Number 30 could be the site of the abbot's lodgings, and it would have to be a fitting place for the reception of important guests. It would therefore include at least a parlour, a bedroom, a dining room and a chapel. The guests' lodgings

Fig. 8 Ewenny. The north gatehouse and wall

(32) could however also have been the site of the abbot's lodgings, and it illustrates how varied the accommodation arrangements in a particular convent could be.

To the east of the church in this case, was the cemetery (31) although there are many instances of important burials taking place in the chapter house. The cemetery was not only the resting place of the monks. The workers who died as a result of accidents whilst building the convent were also laid to rest there.

The whole of the convent or cathedral close was encircled by a high wall with gate houses, which ensured privacy if not a particularly credible means of defence in troubled times. Good enclosing walls have survived at Brecon, Ewenny and St Davids.

The hygienic standards of the monastery were generally in advance

Fig. 9 Usk. The gatehouse

of those of the lay population as a whole, and this is reflected in the attention that was given to water supply and drainage. Careful planning and routing of water channels around important areas such as the rere-dorters, kitchens and farmery is in evidence at several sites, Tintern being a good example. Water mills were operated, and the remains of organized fisheries can still be seen at Cwmhir and Valle Crucis. Monasteries were normally sited by rivers, but Brecon Priory's hilltop position, its robust outward form and its strong containing wall are all reflections of the need also for defence in the troubled border districts. Houses far from the border were also by no means free from trouble, and Strata Florida near Aberystwyth for instance suffered at the hands of Edward I, and later during the rebellion of Owain Glyndŵr

Fig. 10 Tintern. Drainage system next to the kitchen

in 1402. Other minor buildings can often be seen among a monastery's ruins, and it is frequently difficult to deduce their probable functions without a comprehensive ground plan and a knowledge of the chronology of the building programmes through the centuries. The church itself was often subsequently enlarged, sometimes in the aftermath of a fire, and the progressive accumulation of wealth which went hand in hand with a creeping relaxation of the original monastic ideals is often reflected in later extensions and elaborate rebuilds in the latest architectural style which has sometimes obliterated or rendered redundant earlier buildings. Sometimes a flurry of building activity came as a result of an enthusiastic and well-endowed bishop or abbot, and Bishop Gower patronized some of the finest fourteenth-century work in Britain at St Davids. The fabric of Llandaff also benefited greatly from the patronage of Bishop William de Braose who, in the thirteenth century, provided the impressive Lady Chapel at the eastern end of the cathedral. Earl Roger Bigod III financed much of the rebuilding of Tintern's church in the thirteenth century.

The Choir

The monks or canons sat in rows such that they faced each other across the central aisle or crossing space. To the west was a further set of return stalls in a line from north to south such that the stalls faced the choir to the east. These backed onto a solid screen or pulpitum which effectively divided the nave from the choir, and had no specific liturgical function. It either filled the space between the western (or sometimes eastern) crossing piers or was placed across the eastern end of the nave, and it was pierced in the centre by a doorway. The stall immediately to the south of this doorway was usually reserved for the dean in a cathedral and the abbot or prior in a monastic church, and this was often enriched with a more elaborate canopy than its neighbours. Few pulpitums still exist, and those that have survived have often been used as a stand for the organ, as at St Davids, a purpose for which they were never originally intended. The choir stalls were furnished with misericords (from the Latin *misere*: pity, plus *cor*: heart), the medieval equivalent of the old fashioned tip-up cinema seat which provided a ledge for the monk or canon to perch upon whilst attending the long services. The undersides of these were often carved with vigorous scenes, by no means all religious, and here the medieval carver was afforded an excellent opportunity to express himself. The green man, a pagan symbol of fertility which depicted a face from which foliage grew, was a popular subject which had been embraced by the Christian religion. Other subjects included animals both real and legendary, biblical scenes, mermaids, scenes from the Lives of Saints including their martyrdom, jesters, musicians, hunting scenes, and sports. Another favourite subject was a fox dressed in liturgical garb preaching to geese, and this has been interpreted as the established church's caricature of the preachings of the friars with whom they had an uneasy relationship. A fine set of choir stalls and misericords survives at St Davids, and St Asaph Cathedral also has a good set of fifteenth-century stall canopies. The choir stalls at Abergavenny are unique monastic survivors still *in situ* in Wales.

The choir was of course the place where the inhabitants of the monastery spent many hours, and the typical Cistercian timetable began soon after 2am with prayers and psalms, followed by Matins, Lauds, and then Prime at dawn. Then there would follow readings in the cloister, and at around 8am the monks would take breakfast after washing. Then

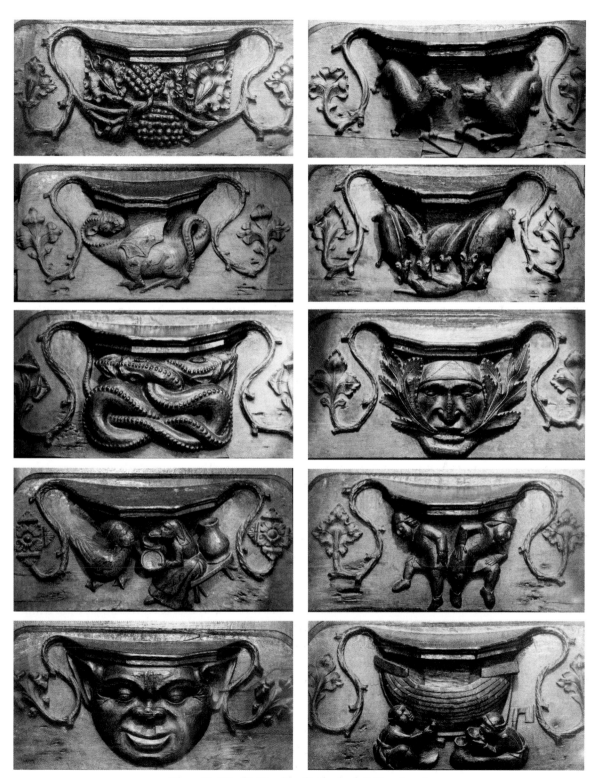

Figs. 11-20 St Davids Cathedral. Misericords

would come Tierce followed by Morrow mass, and at about 9am the chapter house meeting would begin. Following a period of work there would be Sext at noon, followed by High mass, None, and then dinner. At 2.30pm there would be more reading and work, and at 5pm came Vespers. At 6pm in Cistercian houses the abbot would read the Collation in the cloisters before Compline, the last service of the day, and then at 7pm the monks would retire to bed.

A cathedral has a bishop's throne or cathedra (from the Greek *kathedra*: seat) and it is this, the seat of a bishop, which gives the cathedral its name. It was formerly placed in the near vicinity of the high altar such that the bishop faced the choir, but today it is almost always placed just to the east of the south row of the choir stalls facing north.

The sedilia (from the Latin for seats) are a row of three stalls (sometimes more) set against the south wall of the presbytery, traditionally for the use of the priest, deacon and sub-deacon during important ceremonies. Generally of stone, they provided another opportunity for artistic display, and Brecon has a fine thirteenth-century set. Llandaff had a sumptuous nineteenth-century set which have unfortunately been destroyed. Fragments survive, and have been set against the north wall of the south choir aisle, and the quality indicates what a loss there has been.

The piscina (from the Latin word for fish) is a stone basin (with a drain hole) let into the wall to the east of the sedilia for the ceremonial washing of Communion or Mass vessels.

Figs. 21-22 Llandaff. These sedilia fragments date from Prichard's nineteenth-century restoration. An excellent imitation of the late Decorated style, the sedilia contained carvings of a peacock and 'the pelican in her piety' which were designed by Rossetti. It suffered damage and subsequently destruction when alterations were made to the sanctuary

From the thirteenth century double piscinas became common as a result of Pope Innocent III's displeasure at the thought of the priest washing his hands in the same bowl as the holy vessels, but by the fourteenth century single canopies had once more become the norm, perhaps with two small bowls with drain holes underneath. Piscinas can also be spotted in many chapels off transepts, in choir aisles, and elsewhere.

One or two bays further west of the pulpitum was the Rood screen. This was a development of the Rood beam and its purpose was to support the Great Rood or crucifix, flanked by the Virgin Mary and St John the Evangelist. An altar was placed centrally immediately to the west, and two doors pierced the screen, one either side of the altar, so that processions could encircle it. The Rood screen was almost invariably of timber, and was characterized by open tracery and panelling in contrast to the pulpitum wall which was explicitly intended for the isolation of the choir. St Albans Abbey in Hertfordshire has a substantial Rood screen of stone, looking rather like a second pulpitum, but its position and the two doors identify its true nature. Access to the Rood or 'Rood loft' for the purpose of cleaning and the covering of the effigies during Lent was gained by a rood stair or stairs, and the latter can still be seen at Brecon where two doorways now open high up into empty space. Corbels projecting from the walls above them betray the former presence of the Rood. At Valle Crucis the lower part of a stone stairway which may have led up to the Rood can still be seen. The Rood was a dominant feature in all medieval churches, but many of those that did not perish during the Reformation met their end at the hands of Cromwell's Roundheads during the Commonwealth.

The parish churches in Wales can boast a distinguished set of timber screens, dating mainly from the fifteenth and early sixteenth centuries. One of the best known and most elaborately carved is in the

Fig. 23 Penmon. The Norman pedestal piscina

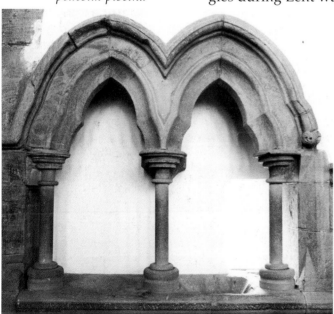

Fig. 24 Brecon. Christ College Chapel. The thirteenth-century double piscina

parish church of Llananno in Powys, fifteen miles south of Newtown. Various such screens are said to have come originally from dissolved monasteries, as certainly happened for example at the parish church of St Nicholas in Montgomery where, in addition to its own screen which faces west, it also sports a second screen behind it facing to the east, together with a set of rather battered stalls and misericords. The second screen and the stalls came from the Augustinian priory of Chirbury just over the border. Other examples are dubious, and it seems that the sight of such magnificent screens in comparatively humble parish churches has prompted a search for a nearby abbey ruin as a probable original home. But this is to do an injustice to the quality of the workmanship often lavished on the interior of the parish church, and a good parallel can be found in East Anglia, a region which is also famous for its splendid timber ceilings and furnishings.

Parclose screens were used to screen off areas of the church to afford a degree of privacy during services. Fourteenth-century timber examples survive to the east of the crossing at St Davids and Ewenny, and a screen which was formerly to the east of the choir at Brecon now encloses St Keyne's Chapel at the eastern end of the north nave aisle.

The Friars
The friars arrived in Britain soon after 1200, but were slow to build their own convents, partly because that would conflict with their refusal to own property, and partly because they were initially given leave to preach in the existing churches. But by the middle of the century there was a need to establish firm bases of their own from which they could work due to swelling congregations and the demand for burials, and also accommodation for libraries and study for which they were renowned. Very little of what they built remains, but the Dominican friary in Norwich in Norfolk is a remarkably complete survivor, and a brief description is merited because it contains the salient features of the houses of both the Dominicans and the Franciscans.

At Norwich, a large aisled nave with a south porch was used by the friars to preach their sermons to the lay-population. Immediately to the east is a passageway known as the walking place, running in a north-south direction along the eastern wall of the nave. One end of this opens onto the streets of the town, and the other end leads to the cloister which will be described presently. If a tower was built it would be placed over this walking place, or sometimes a bellcote would be built. To the east is the choir, rather smaller than the nave as it was used exclusively by the relatively small number of friars themselves. It was fitted with stalls in the manner of an abbey or a cathedral. Christ College Chapel at Brecon was formerly the choir of the Dominican friary of St Nicholas, and some of its stalls survive. The cloister was sometimes not abutted to the wall of the nave as was the case with virtually all abbeys, but separated to create a lane in between the cloister and the nave. Around the cloister the conventual buildings followed no set plan, this being partly as a result of their sighting within an existing town such that they would have to be built where there was room. In common with the abbeys the conventual buildings would often include a dorter, rere-dorter, kitchen, frater with pulpit, cellar, and sometimes guests' lodgings. An important chamber was that kept for the storage of books; the friars were well known not only for their learning but also for their extensive libraries. Much of all this can still be seen at

Norwich today, and the large if somewhat austere nave which is now St Andrew's Hall is evocative of stirring sermons and large, enthusiastic congregations.

The Architecture

The second requirement of architecture is that its buildings must be structurally sound. This not only involves the soundness of the materials used, but also the soundness of the building methods and techniques, including such things as the correct way to use stone and the appropriate use of structural forms such as arches and abutments so that they are capable of supporting such huge structures. It is a large subject, and is covered in chapter five.

The third requirement which is usually asked of architecture is that its buildings should be aesthetically pleasing. This must rank below the other two because, unlike them, it is not mandatory.

Before discussing architectural detail, it is helpful to look briefly at the overall form of the church itself, and where it came from. When the Romans officially adopted the Christian faith, their existing large basilicas — rectangular arcaded exercise and meeting halls lit by aisle and clerestory windows — were the obvious places for holding communal worship. The western Christian church saw no reason to forsake this form as the nave of St Woolos Cathedral in Newport clearly shows, with its two-storey elevations consisting of arches supported by cylindrical pillars, surmounted by simple clerestory windows; and the Romanesque style of the architecture here renders the link with the Roman basilica all the more obvious. As time went on and styles developed, the basilican form became obscured by other strong architectural features such as acutely pointed arches, pointed ribbed vaults, and emphasis on vertical bay-by-bay design. In a fully fledged Gothic nave such as at Tintern Abbey, links with the basilica are therefore rather less obvious. But in Bangor Cathedral's nave, built at the end of the Gothic period, simple two-storey elevations of main arcades and clerestories are once again employed, the overt 'horizontality' of the design at odds with Perpendicular ideas, and a clear basilican form has once more emerged.

But there is a second strong feature of the cathedral and abbey church which was absent in the Roman basilica: a prominent central focus, more suggestive of a centrally planned building. The four main arms of the cruciform church are grouped around a central crossing area upon which is built a great tower. Looking at the Byzantine church, the concept of a long narrow nave is absent, and instead a large dome built over the central space is the principal feature of the building, around which are built a series of subordinate structures, often roofed by smaller domes or semi-domes butting against the central block. In contrast to the basilica, therefore, the Byzantine church was a tall, centrally planned structure, and the Christian church evidently appreciated its symbolism. As a consequence, the greater cathedral and abbey church shows the influence of the Roman basilica with its long, narrow nave, but also of Byzantine architecture as evidenced by its central tower supported by nave, chancel and transepts. The fact that the choir was usually placed beneath the tower in earlier times emphasized the importance of this central feature.

Thomas Rickman (1776-1841) was an early pioneer in the rigorous study of Gothic architecture. He systematically studied such things as building layout, arch profiles, pier types, fenestration, decoration, and means of abutment in an attempt to identify trends and stylistic developments which could be applied to buildings in order to establish chronology, among other things. His book of 1817, *An Attempt to discriminate the Style of Architecture in England, from the Conquest to the Reformation*, introduced the terms Early English, Decorated, and Perpendicular, and although this categorization received much criticism both at the time and subsequently, it remains current; and it provides a convenient and easily under-stood terminology when discussing Gothic architecture. The term Gothic was unknown in medieval times, and was in fact coined by the Italian Georgio Vasari who in the sixteenth century applied it as a term of derision, equating medieval architecture with the barbarism of the sixth-century Goths. But the term is still with us and is now taken to include the building period between the late twelfth century and the mid sixteenth or a little beyond. The Gothic Revival or Gothick movement of the nineteenth century was based upon the style of this era.

No building period can be precisely defined in time, but guidelines are possible and these help us to get a feel for stylistic development and continuity. Pre-Conquest architec-ture obviously implies a period up until 1066. But, as has been mentioned, many 'Norman' elements were already present in English architecture well before this date (which however reflected common influences in both Saxon and Norman architecture as much as Norman influence in England), and in both England and Wales pre-Conquest elements persisted afterwards. In Wales particularly, Celtic decoration continued in the north until at least the thirteenth century.

Norman architecture is characterized by the rounded or semi-circular arch, doorway and window, together with robustness of design with an emphasis upon solid masses of masonry. It persisted until the late twelfth century, developing softer, gentler lines with a growing emphasis on elaborate decoration around arches and doorways. The Norman style was based upon the architecture of ancient Rome, but the prominent key-stone at the crown of the arch which was frequently used in Roman buildings to emphasize important openings and entrances is conspicuously absent from Saxon and Norman interpretations of Romanesque. The circle, leading back upon itself, was a symbol of perfection and unity, heaven rather than earth, and when the semicircular arch was adopted in religious archi-tecture there was evidently a decision not to punctuate its pure, continuous curve. During the Elizabethan and Jacobean periods when Christian symbolism and iconography of a Catholic kind was banished in favour of classical themes, the prominent keystone reap-peared. The dates 1066-1193 could be assigned to this style, the latter marking the comple-tion of the nave of Peterborough Abbey in the Norman or Romanesque style. Already there is an ambiguity because this nave was designed decades before it was completed, but it merely underlines the looseness of the classification. The term 'Norman' is also misleading. Many British craftsmen must have collaborated at the outset, and by about 1100 the archi-tecture of Britain had become an amalgam of both Norman and indigenous Saxon styles. Therefore it soon began to depart from the style of Normandy, and the term Romanesque is better.

The rebuilding of Canterbury's choir after the fire of 1174 catalyzed the wide-spread adoption of the pointed arch. It is interesting that the Cistercians had used it earlier in

England, for example in the mid-twelfth-century nave of Buildwas Abbey in Shropshire, which otherwise strikes a robustly Norman note albeit with a Cistercian timbre. It was also employed on a grand scale as a transverse arch in Durham Cathedral's nave early in the twelfth century. Very soon after Canterbury's new choir, from about 1180, Wells Cathedral was begun in a style which departed radically from anything yet seen in Britain with its composite piers of slender shafts, delicately stylized foliage, tall lancet windows and richly moulded arches. It owed very little to Canterbury's choir, and virtually nothing to France. No rounded arch was used anywhere, and even the window splay was abandoned. Soon after, the rebuilding of Lincoln Cathedral was begun (from 1192) again demonstrating the new style with unencumbered virtuosity. This is what Rickman called Early English, and the period can be said to span the dates 1180-1258. The latter date marks the completion of Salisbury Cathedral's nave entirely in the Early English style.

Although Wells, Lincoln and Ripon represented an abandonment of the Norman style in favour of something quite new, other buildings of the time display many characteristics both Romanesque and Early English. Such buildings are termed 'Transitional'; the choir of Canterbury itself can be termed thus, and the great example in Wales is the nave of St Davids Cathedral, with its main arcade of semi-circular arches, tribune of pointed arches, and decoration showing characteristics of both Norman chevron and Early English dogtooth at the same time. Transitional thus spans 1175-1200, the last quarter of the twelfth century, when the old style was as it were reluctantly relinquished in favour of the new in

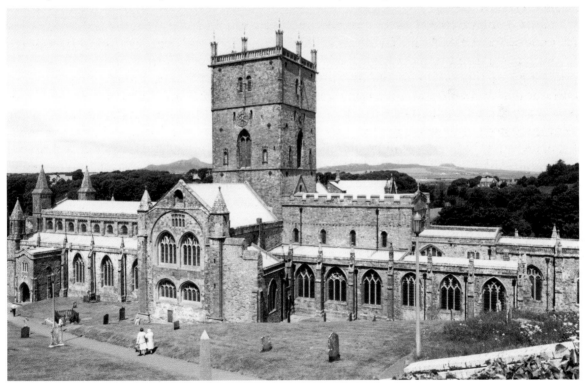

Fig. 25 St Davids Cathedral

certain buildings. The church and west front of Llanthony Priory are another good example with their combinations of pointed and round-headed arcading.

In the 1240s a new type of window tracery was introduced into England from France. Plate tracery, the forming of openings by the appearance of having shapes pierced through solid plates of stone, was already much in evidence as a device for implementing decorative window openings and spandrel decoration in the spaces between arch heads. Henry III, a keen lover of all things French, wanted both a coronation church to rival Rheims Cathedral, and a fitting burial church for Edward the Confessor and the English monarchs, and in 1245 he began the rebuilding of Westminster Abbey in an overtly French style, at least so far as its overall form was concerned. With it came bar tracery: the forming of window designs using individual ribs or 'bars' of stone to create geometric patterns. It had been seen earlier in the 1240s in England at Binham Priory in Norfolk, and possibly also at Netley Abbey in Hampshire, but the high-profile Westminster provided the influence which was rapidly to be felt throughout Britain. Westminster also introduced a naturalistic form of leaf decoration based on recognisable types in contrast to the Early English stiff-leaf, which was a stylized form based upon no particular species. These two features, geometric bar tracery and naturalistic foliage, were characteristic of what has become known as the 'Decorated' style. The other two main features of Westminster Abbey, the very high vault and the re-introduction of the apsidal east end with radiating chapels in the manner of the French *chevet*, did not influence a significant number of later buildings. Geometric bar tracery, that is tracery design based on circles and segments of circles, continued until around 1300, and was then gradually replaced by curvilinear tracery in which the design emphasis was on more free-ranging and sinuous patterns. Just before 1300 the degree of realism achieved in the leaf carving around capitals and elsewhere had reached an almost photographic perfection in Southwell minster's chapter house, and after 1300 it became more stylized and undulating whilst still maintaining considerable focus. The outline of the foliage was now made to conform to the formal shape of a capital or other moulding, rather than being allowed to go its own way.

The Decorated period can be placed between 1245 and 1370, the former date marking the beginning of the rebuilding of Westminster Abbey, the latter the completion of Exeter Cathedral's nave entirely in the Decorated style. This period has been frequently divided into two, Geometric Decorated (1245-1300) and Curvilinear (or Flamboyant) Decorated (1300-1370).

The 'Perpendicular' period, peculiar to Britain, germinated in the 1320s and was first seen on a substantial scale in the chapter house and cloisters of Old St Paul's Cathedral in London, and in St Stephen's Chapel in the palace of Westminster. These buildings have been lost in fires. Emphasis began to be placed upon the vertical line, and window tracery was characterized by mullions which reached straight up until they met the upper curve of the window opening. Blind rectangular panelling was applied to wall surfaces, and window tracery exhibited a strongly panelled characteristic too, this being achieved by the use of transoms — horizontal members dividing the vertical mullions. There was less emphasis on detail, the overall effect being the important consideration. One can imagine the glaziers welcoming the development of panelled window tracery because it provided regular open areas to work with in contrast to the awkward openings which curvilinear tracery produced.

The latter type was in fact short-lived in Britain as the dominant form of tracery, lasting only for about thirty years, and one wonders how much influence and pressure the glaziers exerted. Here was a comparatively rare example of Britain influencing France. French masons took up curvilinear tracery and developed it into a fully flamboyant form, and it continued throughout the fourteenth century and beyond. Later fourteenth-century isolated examples were seen in England and Wales, for example the west window and tower bell-openings of St Asaph Cathedral, and Scotland also favoured it, drawing her influences from the Continent rather than from England with whom she was at war.

The carpenters took to curvilinear reticulated panel work with enthusiasm, and flamboyant examples of their work exist right through to the sixteenth century. St Davids' choir stall panels are a good example of about 1500, and panels from a former parclose screen adorn the pulpit at Brecon. Abergavenny's choir stalls display superb flamboyant panel work in the north bays, the south being a more formal Perpendicular type indicating a different date of carving.

One of the earliest surviving Perpendicular windows is in the south transept of Gloucester Cathedral dating from about 1335. The enormous east window of about 1350, still with most of its original glass, remains the premier example of the sheer audacity of the new style. These windows were created to provide frames for the display of stained glass, but in themselves they rarely look beautiful. Superb examples of the type can be seen in the south transept of Canterbury Cathedral, the same building's west window, King's College Chapel Cambridge, and the already mentioned east window of Gloucester. It is the glass itself which is the *raison d'être*, the tracery affording no attention. One can contrast these examples with the many which have nineteenth-century glass of indifferent or poor quality such as Gloucester's west window, Norwich's west window, and the east window of Bangor. These emphasize how important the glass is if a harsh, depressing effect is to be avoided.

The Perpendicular period can be said to span from 1335 (Gloucester's south transept) to the mid sixteenth century, the dissolution of the monasteries. There are a small number of later buildings in the style. It is a long period, and developments within it included an increasing emphasis on window area as opposed to wall area, delicate panel work, exquisite vaults (e.g. St Davids' Holy Trinity Chapel) and the four-centred depressed arch (Bangor's nave). A Tudor had been on the throne since 1485, and by the dissolution there were marked Renaissance influences such as can be seen in the pendants of St Davids' timber roof.

Dominant throughout all these periods is the use of the arch. The ancient Greeks used post and beam techniques for their buildings, a translation of a style of building in wood into a medium which was in fact ill-suited for it. Wood is strong in tension as well as in compression, and this is put to good use in roofs where tie-beams and kingposts hold the structure together. Stone however is weak in tension, and there are many examples in Greek buildings where the huge horizontal stones spanning the columns have become cracked or have collapsed because their own weight has pulled them apart. Many stone fireplaces of considerably more recent design can be seen to suffer from the same problem. The Greeks knew how to build a perfectly good arch, and sometimes did so, but they preferred the aesthetics of the post and beam. The Romans however recognized that stone must be held in compression if spans of any great width were to be bridged safely, and this necessitated the use of the arch. It was to became the dominant aesthetic motif in religious buildings, but the original reason for its use was in fact a structural one. During the Perpendicular period the arch, structurally, was as necessary as ever, but aesthetically it was to be usurped by the square framing of doorways, and the rectangular panelling of choir stalls, screens, wall surfaces, and of course, window tracery.

The overall developmental trends throughout the whole period are the ever-increasing window areas accompanied by the use of stone more and more as a frame, with more delicate balances of thrust and counter-thrust and judicious buttressing. Bath Abbey, the rebuilding of which was largely complete by the eve of the dissolution, is the archetypal example. Here there are vast areas of glass supported by an array of flying buttresses. One clerestory window on its own lets in more light than many an east or west window elsewhere, and Bath today underlines the vital importance of good stained glass in Perpendicular work by its unfortunate absence here.

The Normans utilized single window openings surrounded by large areas of walling. Time and again one encounters later fenestration to let in more light as it was realized that thrusts could be concentrated in small areas rather than along the whole length of a wall. The Norman shallow clasping pilaster buttress strengthened the wall in its immediate vicinity but did virtually nothing for the overall stability because it increased the wall's footprint area very little. The Early English period is characterized by the lancet window, and groups of these were employed to let in more light whilst still maintaining considerable areas of walling. The more transcendental nature of the pointed arch allowed emphasis to be placed upon verticality, the reaching heavenward combined with a lighter, more ethereal quality. The exteriors of the buildings also became less weighed down aesthetically by masses of masonry, and slender pinnacles and finials were employed to concentrate stabilizing masses in the specific areas where they were needed, in contrast with the earlier Norman technique of providing it everywhere for good measure. Buttresses became more slender but also projected further so as to give a worthwhile increase in footprint area to improve stability. The flying buttress, a kind of half arch which leans against a section of walling, transfers outward thrust from vaults, walls and roofs to the lower parts of the building or to the ground with a delicacy and elegance signalling considerable advances in the understanding of statics. Central towers became more ambitious, but also safer as it was realized that substantial piers and solid walling combined with proper abutment would be needed.

In contrast with France, the British were in the main disinclined to decorate the exteriors of their churches. It is true that we produced many sumptuous towers, and there are a number of splendid west fronts of which Wells is a breathtaking example, but generally the exteriors seem often to have been left to look after themselves. This is a particular characteristic of the Welsh cathedrals and abbeys. St Davids can look quite good in bright sunlight, but in the rain it is dour indeed. The west front is restrained and rather pedestrian. The central tower is high and quite ugly, and one wonders how such an unattractive upper stage could have been added at the same time as the lovely Holy Trinity Chapel was being designed. East of the crossing there seems to have been an excess of building activity, and the various projections are disinclined to compose. Considerable areas of walling are relieved by some attractive window tracery, but this has been restored in a geologically intrusive limestone which is aesthetically unwelcome. None of this prepares us for the considerable delights within, and in this respect St Davids surpasses even Winchester.

Successive building phases within a particular church demonstrate a consistent lack of stylistic compromise. A master mason of the 1330s had no qualms about rebuilding a presbytery very much in the style of his age regardless of the proximity of Norman arches or Early English work, and this stylistic variety characterized many medieval churches. Llandaff is an excellent example. The Norman arch behind the high altar was preserved whilst a late Decorated arcade was provided above. To the east the Lady Chapel is in the early Decorated style, again conceding nothing to the style of the earlier work. The nave is Early English, but the later aisle window openings which were inserted in the fourteenth century are again classic examples of their age with their broad ogee outlines and curvilinear reticulated tracery. The north-west tower of the fifteenth century is archetypically Perpendicular, showing strong affinities with the famous Somerset towers of the period. It is only in the nineteenth century that John Prichard felt obliged to harmonize his south-western tower and spire with the existing Early English work of the west front.

In St Davids there is a rare and rather bizarre example of a mason trying to update an earlier design. St David's Shrine is thirteenth-century work, but one can still see later attempts to add Perpendicular crockets and poppyheads to the arch hood-moulds. This kind of tampering with an earlier design, as opposed to building adjacent to it or demolishing it to make way for the new, is rare indeed.

Fig. 26 Newport. The buildings of St Woolos span a thousand years. On the right is St Mary's Chapel with its pre-Norman walling. On the left is the 80-seater hall which was completed in 1992

The twentieth century has seen the design of W.D. Caröe's stone reredos at Brecon in a beautifully convincing Perpendicular manner, and there is also the architect's son, Alban's, east end at Newport which is unmistakably twentieth century. Yet the disparate styles of St Woolos spanning from pre-Norman times to the 1990s still manage to compose successfully externally as a result of the homogeneity of the colour of the stone throughout the fabric. The modern bricks have been carefully and very sensitively matched in colour to the old stone. Contrast this with the twentieth-century vaulting of the Chapel of St Lawrence in the south transept of Brecon Cathedral. The style is sympathetic to its surroundings, but the geologically intrusive stone prevents it from harmonizing.

The variety of styles which one encounters within these buildings contributes to their interest, and it also suggests that a discussion of the architecture is best approached by taking the buildings as a whole, comparing and contrasting

Fig. 27 Newport. The sanctuary

work of similar build periods in a more or less chronological order which will also illustrate architectural developments throughout the period. The categories Celtic, Norman-Romanesque, Transitional, Early English, Decorated and Perpendicular provide a suitable framework for this, notwithstanding the fact that no precise dates can or should be assigned to each phase, as has been said.

5

Materials and Structural Considerations

The second requirement of architecture, touched upon in the previous chapter and of equal importance to the first, is that its buildings should be safe. By the standards of other medieval buildings the cathedral and abbey churches were enormous structures, rivalled in size only by some of the castles. There were no medieval palaces to compare in scale, and almost all of the other buildings were of timber. It is difficult for us to imagine today what it would have been like to witness the erection of a cathedral in the midst of a medieval town, and in terms of the volume of uninterrupted space which they enclose these churches still comprise some of our largest buildings today. The main characteristic of the buildings being considered is the great sense of solidity and repose. The final Perpendicular phase of the era produced buildings of a delicacy and even serenity which still communicate strength and majesty, and they indirectly tell us something about their builders' lines of thought when the primary requirements of safety, both in terms of a building's statics and in its handling of live loads such as those produced by wind pressure, rain and snow had to be considered.

Medieval building techniques developed empirically. The master mason, who in today's parlance was both the architect and the quantity surveyor, learnt his trade as an apprentice who would then gradually work his way up the hierarchy of his profession. He would gain extensive practical experience of his trade at all levels along the way, and through his own experiences and by studying the successes (and failures) of others he would come to understand the strengths and limitations of the materials he worked with. This not only involved stone. Timber was used in the roofs and floors of these buildings, whilst a great deal of it was also put to use elsewhere during the construction of the church and conventual buildings, and this fact can easily be overlooked. The carpenter played a much larger role in the erection of these stone buildings than is readily apparent from the finished work.

It is often said that travel in medieval times was not indulged in to any great extent, and this is undoubtedly true as far as much of the population was concerned. But many classes of people did travel widely, and for the stonemason a somewhat nomadic life was part and parcel of his trade. Building in stone was reserved for only the most important structures, and as one job was brought to completion the mason would move on to the next which would almost certainly be many miles away.

Although a convent took generations to build, a mason would not spend his entire career in one place, because part of his training included experience with many types of building. There is much evidence to indicate that masons also worked abroad, and the homogeneity of architectural style throughout Britain in any particular decade suggests that there was regular contact and a comparing of notes between the master masons. The Norman or Romanesque style which prevailed until around 1170 was superseded on a country-wide level within a very short time, and when the nave of Peterborough Abbey was completed in the Romanesque style in 1193 it was already architecturally obsolete.

The dogtooth and ballflower motifs appeared in many parts of the country almost at the same time, and the development of window tracery followed a similar pattern throughout the country as a whole. Part of the reason for this was that patrons demanded that their buildings be in the latest style, preoccupations with conservation and stylistic revivals belonging to much later ages. The medieval styles were driven forward by the leading mason architects of their time, many enjoying royal patronage.

The masons shared among their peers information about such things as geometry to generate appropriate building ground plans and elevations, the correct proportions of arches, and the decreasing cross-sectional areas of the tiers of pinnacles for both structural and ascetic reasons. Copies of *The Ten Books on Architecture* by Vitruvius, a renowned Roman architect who flourished in the first century B.C., were in wide circulation. Among descriptions of technical matters such as ordinance, mortar mixes and methods of building walls, Vitruvius also included passages expounding basic sound principles including this one, early in Book 1:

> All these [buildings] must be built with due reference to durability, convenience, and beauty. Durability will be assured when foundations are carried down to the solid ground and materials wisely and liberally selected; convenience, when the arrangement of the apartments is faultless and presents no hindrance to use, and when each class of building is assigned to its suitable and appropriate exposure; and beauty, when the appearance of the work is pleasing and in good taste, and when its members are in due proportion according to correct principles of symmetry.

The buildings which form the subject of this book show time and again how these three fundamental principles were combined to great effect.

Churches frequently reflect stylistic developments as the building progressed, changes along the length of a nave being a good example. This tells us something about both the time scale within which a building was constructed, and the influence of successive master masons between a building's commencement and its eventual completion. It can also indicate pauses in a building campaign pending the availability of further funds.

One frequently hears or reads that a particular patron built a church, a chapel or a nave. For instance, Bishop Gower built much of St Davids' bishops palace, the cathedral's pulpitum, the chapter house, and the south doorway. The charter of Rhys ap Gruffudd of 1184 reads '… I, Rhys, Proprietary Prince of South Wales, have begun to build the venerable abbey entitled Strat-flur; …[Strata Florida].' Bishop Anian II began the re-building of St Asaph Cathedral in the late thirteenth century, and Bernard of Neufmarché, after defeating the Welsh in 1093, built his castle at Brecon and founded St John's Priory. These men certainly patronized, that is obtained the funds for, the erection of the buildings, but it was the master masons in their employ who were the designers and whose job it was to gather together the workforce, skilled and unskilled, which was needed to carry the enterprise through. There are a few instances of patrons taking more than an administrative interest in a project, and occasionally a monk would be skilled in one aspect or another of carpentry or masonry, but these were exceptional cases and a patron's interest in the design and looks of a building rarely extended beyond a stating of a preference for one particular layout rather than another or employing a master mason who had been recommended to him by a colleague.

Who were these master masons? Dr John Harvey and others have conducted a great deal of research into this question, and the names of the masons who were responsible for these buildings, and the extent of their travels, have been identified in many cases. Unfortunately very few names associated with Welsh buildings have come down to us, but we know that Robert Fagan designed St Asaph's tower. Master James of St George was brought from Savoy by Edward I to design his series of castles in north Wales in the late thirteenth century. Work going on in the early fourteenth century in the district encompassing Beaumaris, St Asaph and Valle Crucis shows, with its distinctive window tracery designs accompanied by fairly simple arch profiles with wave mouldings, that an architect of some distinction was designing and influencing building work there. The handling of the pier bases at St Asaph and Valle Crucis is strikingly similar. In south Wales, St Davids Cathedral and Llanthony Priory were being built at the same time in the late twelfth century, and many similarities of design detail strongly suggest the hand of the same architect. St Davids is a lavish building, designed to reflect the status of its bishop who spared little expense. Llanthony was a comparatively minor convent set in the wilds, and it is consequently a much simpler design which few people would have even seen. This reflects the versatility of an architect who was providing that which funds permitted, appropriate to the job in hand.

Surprisingly, the understanding that these buildings were designed by individual master masons, and that important stylistic developments came from men of particular artistic talent, belongs largely to the twentieth century. The master masons were a highly respected and much valued body, and many instances of their wealth and influence among the aristocracy have been cited. For a full discourse, the reader is referred to Harvey's works mentioned in the bibliography, and if we have no impression of the character of these men, perhaps it does not matter. Their personalities endure in their buildings.

Once the site had been chosen, the foundations of the church and conventual buildings could be marked out. Foundations needed to be laid, and this entailed the digging of trenches to a depth of several feet or more which would then be filled with a mixture of mortar and rubble on top of which would be laid large blocks of dressed stone. (Rubble in this context refers to lumps of stone of no particular shape or finish, while dressed stone is that which has been formed into neat blocks with smooth surfaces for the facings of the walls [ashlar], the window tracery, and corner blocks or quoins). Walls could be built entirely of rubble or faced with ashlar,

Fig. 28 Lamphey. Ashlar facing on a rubble core

51

whilst ashlar was normally used for the quoins. Rubble-built walls were usually plastered over inside, and often outside as well.

Sometimes the site would be found to be boggy or to contain a high concentration of clay, both of which can cause problems in term's of a building's stability. In the former case a raft consisting of logs would be laid beneath the foundations, and in the latter case a more thorough excavation for the foundations would need to be carried out. Piles were sometimes driven into the ground. Clay tends to ooze out from beneath foundations under the great weight of the superstructure causing settlement or subsidence, and adequate precautions were not always taken to avoid this. One sometimes sees problems of this sort in the vicinity of the crossing where the weight of the tower has caused the supporting piers to sink further than the adjacent arcades, a spectacular example of which can be seen at Selby Abbey in Yorkshire, the result of a high water table only a few feet below ground level. The leaning arcades at St Davids are the result of building on clay within the near vicinity of a river, a sloping site aggravating the problem. St Asaph is also built on clay, and in the 1930s the area below the central tower had to be underpinned with cement and steel girders. The work was carried out by C.M. Oldrid Scott, grandson of Sir George Gilbert Scott, about whom more will be told later.

After the foundations the plinth could be built, this being the section of wall immediately above ground level. It was sometimes splayed outwards to form what is called a batter in order to give additional strength to the bottom section of the wall, and also to help protect it from the elements. The walls were often of double-skin construction, that is there would be an outer and an inner wall, the cavity in between being filled with a mixture of mortar and rubble. This filling economized on the use of dressed stone, and it also formed a less than totally rigid bond which would allow a certain amount of movement or drift of a wall as a whole under the influence of various loads imposed upon it as the building settled. The height of the wall could be raised to about head height quite easily without the cost of scaf-

folding at this stage. Many walls were built entirely of rubble with the exception of corner reinforcements and openings, this again saving on cost.

Once the foundations and lower courses of walling were in place, it was customary to continue building the east end of the church from this stage first so that the choir, transepts and the eastern bay or two of the nave could be completed as soon as possible. The church would then be consecrated, and services could begin. The nave was usually built later, and a

Fig. 29 St Davids Cathedral. Buttresses supporting the north wall of the nave

pause in the building programme here is sometimes indicated by the fact that the eastern bay or bays of the nave can be seen to be of a different design from the rest of the nave, as for instance at Llandaff and Llanthony. The eastern bay would be constructed to act as a kind of flying buttress to support the transepts and the lower section of the central tower (which would often be completed last of all) so that the building could be safely left pending the continuation of the nave at a later date. Unfinished walls would be covered with thatch to protect them from water penetration and frost damage. Attention could then be concentrated on the important conventual buildings such as the chapter house, fraters and dorters. The master mason himself would draw up the plans from which his subordinate masons would work, and he would provide full-sized templates for mouldings of capitals and bases of piers, window tracery design, arch profiles, and designs for the ornamental carving. He would inspect the quarry from which the stone was brought, and it was frequently the case that blocks of stone were dressed and carved at the quarry before transportation to the building site. Some types of stone are rather soft when first quarried due to the presence of quarry sap: moisture in the stone which gradually evaporates, accompanied by a 'consolidating' or hardening up of the stone. Carving the stone in its 'green' state is easier because the stone is softer. The terms green and sap are borrowed from the timber industry of course. It also made good sense because the transportation of stone was (and is) an expensive business, and a great deal of stone is chiselled away and discarded during the carving of arch voussoirs, tracery, capital mouldings and columns. However, much detailed carving would be carried out on the building site, to ensure that the intricately carved shapes would piece together to fit the structure. Design changes and adjustments as the work progressed were not infrequent, and it was important that the team working on its various components were in close touch with each other.

The more junior masons would frequently be employed on a piecework basis to produce the blocks of stone, and each one would have his own mark which he would incise on the piece of stone which he dressed to indicate that it had been his work. A mason could not use a mark until he was fully qualified. Such masons' marks can be seen in many places in cathedrals, abbeys and castles, and an appendix explores the subject in a little more detail. The more complicated carving such as capitals and window tracery was executed by more experienced masons, who would be paid on a per day or job basis. Their marks were therefore not needed on the stone, although one does very occasionally find them on tracery and the other more intricately carved work. The master mason's own mark would never appear on stone, but sometimes he put his mark next to his signature when contracts were drawn up. If he had time to do any of the actual carving at all, he would quite naturally reserve the plum jobs for himself, for example the pulpitum, tomb canopies, or effigies. In contrast with the fairly simple mouldings for window tracery and doorways which would be carved in quantity for the building by the jobbing masons, the more intricate carving such as for statues, decorated capitals and roof bosses would take a considerable time to produce. For instance it could take several weeks for a mason to carve a delicately foliated stiff-leaf capital.

It would generally take perhaps two decades to complete the choir, transepts, and the eastern bay or bays of the nave. The master would therefore have several building projects under his supervision simultaneously, often in different parts of the country. When the time came to continue the nave, the original designer could very well be retired or dead. A new mason would be brought in and, as has already been mentioned, he would usually continue the work in a modified style of his own. The church at Tintern Abbey was completely rebuilt in the comparatively short space of thirty years, but even here stylistic changes are encountered as the building progressed, betraying the hands of at least three architects.

The completion of the church would generally be achieved somewhere between thirty and eighty years after it was begun, but the time-scale could vary considerably. The continuing availability or otherwise of funds dictated the progress of the building programme, and this has also been the case in more recent times. One can see how Giles Gilbert Scott altered the design of the nave of Downside Abbey in Somerset when its building continued under his supervision. The nave was completed in 1925. The same architect designed Liverpool Anglican cathedral, and he died in 1960 eighteen years before it was completed. Guildford Cathedral was consecrated in 1961 before the central tower was built.

The carpenters provided the scaffolding necessary to carry walls upwards beyond head height. Poles of suitable timber such as fir would be lashed together, and timber supports known as putlogs were inserted horizontally into putlog holes left in the masonry in order to support the working platforms. A great number of these holes can be seen on the interior and exterior walls of Tintern Abbey's church. It was also the job of the carpenter to provide false work and centring for walls, arches, doorways and windows: timber profiles to support the masonry above the openings which would be left in place until the mortar had set. It was the usual practice to construct a small number of arches at a time, so that the same centring could then be used again to support the next group. Machinery for the hoisting of the blocks of stone up to the working platforms would also be provided by the carpenters, and they would play an important part in the design and construction of the ribbed vaulting in the aisles and across the main roof spans. Timber mock-ups were assembled on the ground before the masons copied the design in stone, but sometimes the final vault would be of timber, such as those seen at St Asaph, St Davids, and in the cloisters of Lincoln Cathedral. When it came to planning the roof the carpenter would choose appropriate trees, preferably oak, for the job. The maximum spans of the nave, transepts and presbytery were dictated by the availability of timber which would reach across, and the mason had to bear this in mind when choosing his dimensions at the initial design stage. A flat ceiling spanning the main widths of the building was an alternative often preferred to stone or timber vaulting, and St Davids' nave has a magnificent example dating from the early sixteenth century. The hammer-beam roof was another favoured form and there is a good mid-sixteenth-century one at St Idloes Church in Llanidloes, Powys. The panelled wagon roof over the chancel of St Silin's Church at Llansilin in Clwyd is another notable example of the medieval carpenter's skill, as is the magnificent arch-braced panelled roof of about 1500 at St Collen's in Llangollen.

Few parish churches have stone vaults, and reasons of cost have often been suggested. But the above-mentioned timber ceilings could hardly be regarded as cheap expedients, and there was another reason to roof in wood. The large abbey church or cathedral could spend years vaulting an arm of its building, there being plenty of room elsewhere for the church's business to continue. It would be vaulted in sections in this way. The somewhat smaller parish church was a different matter. To vault a nave would effectively close the church for years while the work was being done. A wooden roof however could be made and trial assembled on the ground at a place remote from the site; the joints would then all be marked up and the roof dismantled and brought to the church where it would be installed in a short space of time, causing minimum disruption to the church's business. This necessity as much as anything else is responsible for the magnificent timber roofs.

Towers were always intended to support spires of one sort or another until the end of the fourteenth century, and spire building still continued in later centuries. Many of these were of timber, and the loss of almost all of them again encourages us to underestimate the carpenters' contribution. One

Fig. 30 Brecon Cathedral. This cresset stone is the largest example known in Britain. Tallow was poured into the cups, and the burning wicks which were placed in them must have produced an impressive pool of light

of the main incentives to vault in stone though was as a precaution against fire. The lightning conductor was not invented until late in the eighteenth century, and there are many cases where lightning strikes caused devastating fires. York Minster with its timber vault succumbed only a few years ago. A stone vault would protect the church from the burning timber roofs above, although the lighting of the church with candles, cresset stones and lamps was another fire hazard from within. Choir stalls and other furnishings were provided by the carpenters, and St Davids' impressive bishop's throne and set of stalls have already been mentioned.

The pitched roof was itself in earlier times covered with thatch or shingles, but lead sheeting became the norm from the twelfth century. The plumber was thus a vital member of the team, although slate was also used.

The blacksmith was another important member of the building team. There would be a constant stream of masons' chisels to be kept sharp, and new tools would need to be provided regularly. Doors were usually reinforced with iron strapping, and some beautiful examples of these

*Fig. 31 Brecon Cathedral.
The north transept door*

have survived. The door leading into the north transept at Brecon Cathedral is a good thirteenth-century example, and there are others where the timber has been renewed several times over the centuries whilst the original ironwork has been retained. There were also locks and hinges to be made, and of course nails. Iron cramps were used to tie together blocks of stone in critical areas such as towers, spires, finials and pinnacles which were particularly vulnerable to wind stresses, as these needed a firm anchor. The cramp would be inserted into a prepared hole in the stone and then molten lead would be poured in to encase the iron in order to protect it against rusting. Over the centuries the lead has failed in many instances and the iron has expanded as it rusted, splitting the stone. One task of the restorers of these buildings has been to replace iron with stainless steel.

The glaziers had considerable areas of window to fill. Much of the raw glass came from France because the particularly pure sand needed was available in the Fontainebleau area, and so France developed a flourishing glass industry, which continues to this day. It wasn't until the later medieval period that Britain began to produce glass in quantity, although English glass dating from Saxon times has been found. The strips of lead holding the individual panes of glass together are shaped so that their cross-section forms a capital H to provide two grooves into which the glass could be slotted and gripped. The strips are called *cames*. Lead is a very soft metal and will not support large areas of glass unaided, and so vertical and horizontal iron rods (respectively stanchions and saddle bars) were fitted into the window openings at intervals to lend additional support.

Building Stone

The stone would come from the nearest convenient source, the more local the better, but sometimes good building stone was not available in a particular district. South-east England and East Anglia were poorly served, and the Normans brought stone from the Isle of Wight to build Chichester Cathedral, and from Caen in Normandy to build Canterbury and Rochester for example. Peterborough and Ely Cathedrals were built with Barnack stone from near Peterborough, but such was the difficulty of transporting it over the waterlogged fens that Norwich Cathedral was built with both Caen and Barnack stone. Transportation by sea and inland waterways was cheaper than by land, and even in recent times Portland stone from the Dorset coast could be bought more cheaply in Dublin than in the English Midlands.

The band of sandstone which stretches across mid Wales and through western England towards Chester was quarried to build Brecon Cathedral, Llanthony Priory, and Tintern Abbey. Bands of limestone were quarried to build Llandaff Cathedral, Kidwelly, Margam, Neath and Ewenny. St Davids Cathedral is built with Caerbwdy Grit. A grit is a sandstone with angular particles, and here the mineral Feldspar is present in the stone. Anglesey limestone was used to build Penmon Priory and Caernarfon Castle in the north.

Types of Stone

It is the sedimentary rocks — limestone and sandstone — formed from multiple layers or strata of material deposited over the course of millions of years, which provide the bulk of the building stone in Britain.

Limestone consists principally of calcium carbonate, and the binder or matrix which cements the strata together usually consists of calcite crystals. Sometimes magnesium carbonate, dolomite, is present in the matrix, and minerals such as glauconite, a complex iron/potassium mineral, give rise to the various distinctive colourings. Glauconite lends a green hue to much building stone in Wales and western England. Sandstone consists principally of silicon dioxide: silica or quartz. The matrix can be of virtually pure quartz to form a particularly tough sandstone, or of calcite or dolomite. Iron oxides also play a large part in the matrix of many sandstones, giving them their characteristic red or lilac hue.

The other two forms of rock are igneous and metamorphic. The latter is formed from an already existing rock as a result of great pressure, sometimes also accompanied by heat, which transforms one type of rock into another. True marble is a metamorphic rock, and slate is another example which continues to be important as a roofing and cladding material. Igneous rock is formed by the solidification of molten rock deep in the earth (magma) or volcanic lava. It is therefore not stratified, and so consideration of the lie of the bed (discussed presently) when it is used as a building stone is not relevant. Granite is a typically hard, intractable example which has been a common building stone in Devon, Cornwall (Truro Cathedral will outlast them all), and in parts of the English Midlands. There is also much granite in Scotland, and Clwyd has yielded a small amount. To a stonemason, 'rock' becomes 'stone' when it has been detached from the face of the quarry.

Different types of stone have shown marked variations in weathering properties over the centuries. Generally, limestone has lasted longer than sandstone, but there have been exceptions to this. The principal factor in a stone's ability to stand up to erosion is the nature of the matrix that binds the strata of the stone together. Portland stone from the Dorset coast is a very pale, pure form of limestone with a calcite matrix which contains few impurities. As a result, the ability of the matrix to crystallize and bond with the stone was unencumbered by the presence of other substances, and Portland is as a result one of our toughest limestones, surviving for centuries even in polluted cities. The thirteenth-century limestone west front of Llandaff Cathedral has stood up well over the centuries, albeit with the help of restorations, and the twelfth-century south doorway is also in excellent condition. The west door at Strata Florida is another example which has weathered very well.

These can be contrasted with the sandstone west front of St Davids Cathedral which, even after only 150 years or so, is showing marked signs of erosion. The feldspar and other mineral impurities present in the matrix of the stone prevent a tough, continuous crystalline structure from forming, and the stone erodes comparatively quickly as a result. The decaying sandstone arch at Basingwerk is also a good place to see how the binding matrix of the stone has been eroded away over the centuries through the action of water running through the surface of permeable stone. Some sandstones however stand up very well. The west door at Chepstow Priory, built using a local sandstone, still exhibits crisp carving after over eight hundred years of exposure, and the stonework at Llanthony Priory has again stood up well. Some types of millstone grit sandstone can be almost as hard as granite.

Some limestones have proved to be quite poor with respect to their susceptibility to erosion, and a well-known example is the Reigate stone from the south of London which was used to build Westminster Abbey. Erosion was so bad that much of the exterior of the building has had to be refaced with alternatives.

One might ask, therefore, why the toughest stone available from other regions should not be used for the restoration of these buildings. But this would be to rob them of their local identity and character. One of the pleasures of visiting Britain's medieval buildings, and particularly those of Wales, is the way in which they seem to belong to the land, fully in harmony with their surroundings. The same textures and hues can be seen in the surrounding buildings, in the stone walling of the farms, and in the surrounding rocks. The limestone window tracery at St Davids will undoubtedly last longer than the original sandstone, but it simply looks out of place. It does not belong here.

When it comes to using stone for building, it is helpful to look upon a block as if it were a deep pile of A4 writing paper, each sheet representing a layer of sediment or strata. The matrix cements each sheet to the one above and below. Place the pile on the floor and stand on it. It is immensely strong in compression. But stand the pile up on its end and try standing on it again. The sheets split apart and the block disintegrates. Stone is of course considerably tougher than this, but the principle is exactly the same. Understandably, the master mason would want to use the stone in compression, when it would be termed 'naturally bedded' or 'in bed'. Thus, when the stone was quarried, the bed was marked so that the masons can orientate it correctly; sometimes with very fine-grained examples it is difficult to determine the lie of the bed. (Strata can lie in any direction in the ground, not just horizontally, as the result of movement of the earth's crust over millions of years.) Weathering of stone will often remove part of the matrix at the surface, and a close look at an external wall of ashlar is often rewarded by the sight of horizontal bands running along the blocks which is indicative of the lie of the bed. These are not to be confused with tooling marks which can run in any direction. Very occasionally, one spots a block with the bed incorrectly orientated vertically, or 'edge bedded', and the block will often be seen to be weathering at a more rapid rate than those surrounding it due to the downward forces splitting the stone, as was the

Fig. 32 St Davids Cathedral. Vertically bedded stone splitting under pressure

case with the upturned pile of A4 paper. Sometimes one also sees a column splitting along its length, the result of pressure on vertically bedded stone. The golden rule is that the pressure exerted on a block, from whatever direction, should endeavour to compress the strata firmly together.

The voussoirs of an arch, that is the individual wedge-shaped stones which together form the curve, need to be considered carefully with respect to the lie of the bed in order that the force exerted on the strata of each stone is appropriately compressive. The arch at the eastern end of the church's south aisle at Basingwerk Abbey ruin is in a fairly advanced state of decay, and the exposed strata of the sandstone affords an excellent opportunity to study the correct lie of the bed for each voussoir (Fig. 33). In fact, a ruin is a very good place to study masonry because one can see aspects of the constructional techniques which are not normally exposed in a building in use. The walling above the arch exerts a downward thrust which is transmitted by the voussoirs down towards the ground. Each voussoir is in compression, and the bed must be orientated to take account of this. As can be seen, in the top voussoirs the bed is nearly vertical, and as we look at successive voussoirs we see that

Fig. 33 Basingwerk. The arch in the south nave aisle showing the rock's bedding planes under compression in the voussoirs

the bed progressively assumes a more horizontal position until it *is* horizontal at the point of springing of the arch. All the voussoirs are therefore loaded by the weight above such that the strata are compressed together to produce a strong, stable structure.

Coping stones, that is stones which form the top of a wall such as crenellations or battlements, bear no weight from above but pressure is exerted from the blocks to each side. The bed is therefore orientated vertically (edge bedded) such that the edges of the strata face to the front and back, their faces butting up against the adjacent stones so that the strata are again under compression. 'Face bedding', orientating a block with the face of the strata exposed as a vertical section of wall is a poor building technique because rain can penetrate behind the bedding planes and undermine the matrix. This causes flaking of the stone as the surface layers lose their binding, and of course weight from above also tends to split the strata apart. The only type of face bedding which is employed is when stone is used for pavements and stair treads such that the weight from above from traffic tends to compress the strata together, as was the case when you stood on the pile of A4 paper. This is another application of natural bedding.

Mortar
The stones are bound together with mortar, which is principally a mixture of lime and sand. A digression into the chemistry of lime will give an appreciation of how remarkable was the empirical nature of its discovery, as the precise chemistry was not worked out until the nineteenth century. Yet it was used in Roman times, and even well before that.

Lime is calcium hydroxide. It is produced by heating calcium carbonate, a convenient source of which is limestone or chalk, to a temperature of between 800 and 1,000 degrees

Celsius. The calcium carbonate decomposes into calcium oxide or *quicklime* and carbon dioxide gas. The heat was formerly provided either by wood-burning lime kilns or a simpler arrangement of layers of wood and stone which is then set on fire. The calcium oxide produced is a very reactive substance, and it is dangerous to handle. It reacts with the water vapour and carbon dioxide in the air, and so must be stored in air-tight bags. The lumps of calcium oxide or quicklime produced are then tipped into a trough of water, with which they vigorously

Fig. 34 Porthclais, St Davids. A plaque states that these limekilns were in use between about 1650 and 1900, and that some of the lime produced was used for mortar. Most of the production was spread on the fields to neutralize the acids in the soil. Wood was loaded into the draw-holes in the sides, and the single large cones in the top were packed with limestone. They are about twelve feet high

react, to produce calcium hydroxide or slaked lime. Slaked lime, also known as hydrated lime or just lime, is slightly soluble in water, and it is also slightly caustic. The lime is pressed through a sieve to remove impurities such as odd pebbles and unslaked lumps of quicklime, and then stored in a tank or lime pit under a layer of water to prevent contact with the air. The texture and appearance of the pure white lime are like thick cream, and this mixture of calcium hydroxide and water is called lime putty.

Upon exposure to the air the lime slowly reacts with the carbon dioxide present, and so turns back into the calcium carbonate from which it was originally formed, completing a cycle. This is called carbonation.

Lime is weak after it has dried to become hard, but the calcium carbonate which it goes on to form is very tough. The high water content of lime putty means that if it is used on its own as a mortar the loss of the volume of water as it dries causes considerable shrinkage and cracking, so a mixture of lime and sand is used, the latter being an inert aggregate to provide a volume filler whilst taking no part in the subsequent carbonation process. Lime alone is sometimes used for very fine joints. The lime to sand ratio in the medieval period was generally in the order of 1:3 or 1:4, that is one part of lime putty to three or four parts of sand. During the Norman period a generally higher proportion of lime was used in the mix.

The Romans required a cement capable of setting under water, which they could use for their water engineering works: the Roman baths and aqueducts. Ordinary lime and sand will not do so. They discovered that the burning of limestone which had a high clay content to produce quicklime would subsequently slake to produce a lime which chemically set hard without the need for aerial carbonation over a period of time, and this hydraulic lime is so called because it will set even under water. It is the aluminium oxide in the clay which reacts chemically with the lime to form a set. The Romans also discovered that adding a type of volcanic ash powder from the region of Pozzuoli near Naples to ordinary lime would also produce the same effect. Other sources of the powder were subsequently discovered, and again it was the aluminium oxide present which reacted with the lime.

It is fascinating that a three-stage process of burning limestone followed by slaking to produce lime, which would subsequently harden by a chemical reaction, should be determined empirically with no knowledge at all of the chemistry involved. One can imagine observations being noted of the effects of heat on blocks of limestone which were used to make fireplaces, turning them into something with rather different properties. Pouring on of water to douse the flames and cool the blocks would then slake them to produce lime which, if left, would gradually revert to the original limestone from whence it came. Receptive minds would have noticed this, and put it to good use. The later development of hydraulic lime suggests liberal amounts of trial and error in the search for new mixes, and in Britain and elsewhere during the Middle Ages there are instances of all manner of things being added to the mix such as urine, egg-whites, and ox blood. Some of these things do indeed contain substances which will react with the lime, and the familiar clotting of blood obviously led to experiments in using it to help form a firm set.

A picture has been built up of the level and variety of activity at the site of the building. Temporary timber structures to provide masons' lodges and other workshops would be grouped next to the site, and provisions and lodgings would need to be found. These were not easily procured when a Cistercian house was being established many miles from the nearest town, and it must be remembered that the building of a church and convent was a long term project.

Tiles were produced in large quantities at several sites, and quite a variety can be seen in Figures 35-38.

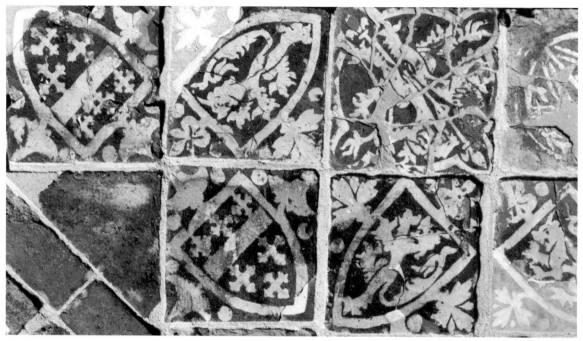

Fig. 35-36 Neath (above and previous page). Encaustic tiles. Such tiles date mainly from the thirteenth and fourteenth centuries. A wooden die carrying the design in relief was pressed into the clay, and the resulting imprint was then filled with a light coloured clay before firing. They were produced in large quantities, and identical designs are found in many abbeys

Fig. 37-38 Strata Florida. Encaustic and incised tiles. On the right is seen an enigmatic 'man with a mirror'. It may show a warrior holding a shield, but the way he holds it out in front of him suggests that it could be a Disc of the Lamb of God (Agnus Dei) which came into use several centuries before the tile was made. There are many depictions of the Lamb set within a circle in religious art

Structural Principles

The church was a building which remained standing for many years with minimal maintenance, performing its function in an unobtrusive manner. All the various thrusts and pressures exerted were generally contained within the fabric of the church itself. Walls are simple

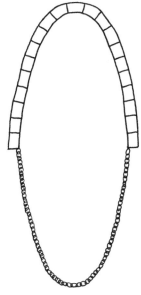

Fig. 39 A catenarian arch, the mirror image of a chain's course when hung between two points

structures, the piling of stone upon stone requiring only a firm foundation. The latter could prove inadequate as we have seen, but in the main there were no problems. An arch is different. It exerts both a downward and an outward thrust, and the appropriate handling of these two forces had again been determined empirically: experience and observation counted for much in an age before rigorous calculations of such things had become possible. The ideal shape of an arch from a structural point of view follows what is known as a catenarian curve (Figure 39). It can be determined by hanging a chain between the two points of springing of the arch, the length of chain being that which produces the required height of the arch. The mirror image of the shape the chain assumes under gravity, the catenary curve, gives the ideal shape of the arch structurally, ensuring that each voussoir is in compression and that the lines of downward and outward force are contained within them. The ideal shape of the curve is modified by the weight of the structure which the arch has to bear. Comparatively few arch profiles fit this ideal, the arch profile of the fan vaulting above King's College Chapel in Cambridge being one exception which allowed quite thin blocks of stone to be used which nevertheless still contained the lines of thrust within them. The exact mathematical details of the catenarian curve were worked out by Robert Hooke only in the seventeenth century.

A semi-circular Norman or Romanesque arch gives the appearance of being a robust structure, this being helped by the generally fortress-like style of the architecture of the time with its emphasis on sheer mass of stone as a means of achieving stability. By definition, a semi-circular or round-headed arch has a height equal to half of its span, and this was a limitation with respect to bay and vaulting design since only one single height can be obtained from a given span if a complete arch is to be used. This arch profile departs from the catenary ideal considerably, and there is little margin for error in its construction. If the outward thrust which it exerts pushes the supporting piers apart to any great extent during settlement the keystone at the crown of the arch is soon in danger of dropping out, precipitating the collapse of the whole arch, and the emphasis on solid mass in this style of architecture was what held the buildings up rather than an understanding of thrusts and counterthrusts. This is reflected also in the window openings. There was a reluctance to weaken the walls unduly with large areas of fenestration, and Norman buildings are characterized by their single round-headed windows surrounded by large areas of masonry. Their barrel or tunnel vaults distributed weight evenly along the lengths of walling, whereas later ribbed vaults tended to concentrate thrusts in specific areas. The earlier masons were disinclined to take any chances.

The pointed arch became fashionable in Britain after the rebuilding of Canterbury Cathedral's choir after a bad fire in 1175. It had been used elsewhere in Europe before, for example in parts of Spain and Sicily which were subject to Moorish influences, and in France earlier in the twelfth century. It more nearly fits the catenary ideal, and it has the added advantage that its height is independent of its span. The height can be varied at will to produce the acutely pointed profile of the lancet arch, Figure 40, or the somewhat squatter obtuse arch, Figure 41, or of course any profile in between. The taller the arch compared with its span, the more the thrust will be concentrated in a downward direction rather than outwards. This predominantly downward projection of force in a lancet arch can be appreciated by looking at Figure 40. The arch profile in Figure 41 exerts considerably more outward thrust as is indicated by the accompanying triangle of forces. In the later Gothic period the four-centred or depressed arch, depressed because its height is considerably less than half of its span, was employed, and this exerts considerable outward thrust requiring careful abutment (Figure 42). It is 'four centred' because the curve is made up of four separate arcs of circles which are struck from four distinct centres.

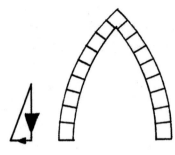

Fig. 40 The proportions of a lancet arch

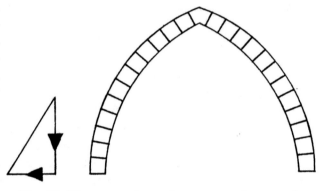

Fig. 41 The proportions of a squatter obtuse arch

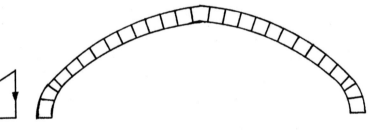

Fig. 42 The proportions of a depressed arch

The crossing space of a church where the nave, choir and transept arms meet is in fact a rather daring application of the balance of forces. The four large crossing arches support the central tower, and the weight of the latter causes considerable outward thrust from the arches which exerts force on the supporting piers in an outward direction. The counter-thrusts of the arcades and walls of the four arms of the church counterbalance this to maintain equilibrium. The tower itself rests on just the four crossing arches and their piers, and there is nothing directly underneath. This delicate balance was not always successful, and central towers were a cause of much concern during the period and have been since.

The thrust of the nave arcades at St Davids began to push the west front over, and remedial action had to be taken in the eighteenth and nineteenth centuries. The problems at the crossing area of this cathedral are a good illustration of what can arise. The tower collapsed in 1220, falling towards the east and bringing down the upper sections of the presbytery walls with it. The exact cause is not known, but a combination of inadequate supporting piers, faulty tower construction and possibly also an earthquake is likely. Many towers collapsed during the hundred years or so after the Norman Conquest: Winchester's went in 1107 less than a decade after it was finished. Beverley's collapsed in 1200 whilst it was still being built. The so-called earthquake which destroyed much of Lincoln Cathedral in 1185 is more likely to have been a collapsing central tower since the west front and the adjacent castle were unharmed. Chichester's tower and spire survived until 1861 when the crossing piers eventually buckled and the spire telescoped downwards into the crossing area. The present tower and spire are a nineteenth-century replica. A common factor in many of these disasters is the method of the construction of the walling already described, that is a double skin with the intervening cavity filled with rubble — stone and mortar. Crossing piers were constructed like this both during the Norman period and a little after, and so the weight of the tower bears down on the crossing arches and thence to the outer ashlar skin and infilling of the piers. Over a period of time the infill settles and the weight is transferred more and more towards the outer facings which are an inadequate support on their own. Careful probing into the cores of the crossing piers at Salisbury has revealed that they are constructed from good blocks of dressed stone throughout their thickness, and it is difficult to imagine how the enormous tower and spire could still be standing after nearly seven hundred years if it were otherwise. At Lincoln the rubble-filled cores of the crossing piers were injected with cement in the 1920s to consolidate them, and similar measures have recently been taken at Worcester.

But masons learnt from their mistakes, and apart from the adoption of solid pier construction they began to take extra precautions regarding the construction of the tower itself. It became common practice to build only perhaps a ten-foot section of the tower during a season; the tops of the walls were then thatched over to protect them from water and frost penetration, and the work was then left to develop signs of worrying settlement before the next section was built during the following year. In this way, problems could be identified early and appropriate action taken.

Problems at St Davids
A return to St Davids gives an opportunity both to look at some specific problems and to gain an insight into the kind of work needed to keep these buildings standing. Sir George Gilbert Scott (1811-78), an architect active as a designer of both religious and secular buildings, as time went by devoted his energies more and more to the restoration of churches and cathedrals, including those of Bangor, Brecon, St Davids and St Asaph. If his work is sometimes regarded as punitive and inappropriate that at St Davids was generally careful and sympathetic. His report to the Dean and Chapter of 1869, from which extracts are quoted below, provides an insight into the building practices of the Gothic age:

> … while the entire building was reported to be in a state of the most severe dilapidation, and some portions actually in ruins, the greatest immediate danger was to be apprehended from the tower, the crushed condition of two of those sustaining piers rendered its fall an event by no means improbable … I have never met with a case so

serious, and involving so great an amount of apparent and actual danger, as that of your Cathedral; for not only is the tower far larger and of vastly greater weight than any other on which I have been called to operate, but its two western piers were more alarmingly shattered than anything I have witnessed elsewhere. ...

The western piers consist each of two portions, the parts towards the nave belonging to De Leiâ's work of the twelfth century, and those towards the transepts having been added after the catastrophe of 1220. Of these, the older of the western portions are literally, at least so far as they are open to examination, shattered to fragments, and the same process has extended itself in a less degree into the later or eastern parts of each pier; in fact, the only security which the tower has from actually falling, is the buttressing it sustains from the walls of the transepts and the nave, though the latter have themselves severely suffered under the undue pressure thus brought upon them.

... the object to be aimed at was little (if anything) less than the rebuilding from their foundation of two of the four piers which sustained the tower, each of them bearing a load of 1,150 tons, which had to be supported by timber shoring during the operation.

Our first work, however, was to take measures for binding together, and otherwise strengthening the tower itself, so as to avoid the danger of its becoming fractured, or otherwise injured, during the reconstruction of its supporting piers; and this was rendered the more necessary by the disintegrated state of the tower walls immediately resting on the lower arches, and the enormous cracks by which the north and south walls were rent throughout their entire height. This object was attained by the introduction of permanent iron ties of great strength, at several different levels, binding all the walls together; by the use of temporary girders and massive timber-work round the exterior of the tower, throughout the greater part of its height; and by repairing with new stone and strong cement many parts of the disintegrated walls.

The shoring by which the weight of the western half of the tower has been temporarily supported is of three descriptions – 1st, direct supports under the western, northern and southern arches (the two former consisting of timber framing, and the latter being provided by an old stone wall, by which the arch was blocked), 2ndly, vertical shores of immense strength, supporting 'needles', or horizontal masses of timber, passing through the walls; and 3rdly, by 'raking' or inclined shores abutting against the walls in all directions, and both supporting weight and preventing lateral motion. ...

Mr. Clear, the Clerk of Works, and myself, foreseeing some difficulty, arranged a plan by which, before cutting through the wall [of the tower], a sort of tunnel of strong stone should be formed through it, by inserting the stones, one at a time, in the shattered rubble work, and then removing the enclosed wall. This was done, with some difficulty, to a depth of 2 feet from either side, but as the wall is 6 feet thick, there remained 2 feet in the middle untunnelled, and when the enclosed wall was attempted to be removed, the middle mass began to pour out like an avalanche, which was only stopped by the immediate insertion of sand-bags, and by subsequently running the wall from above with liquid cement, and thus solidifying the disintegrated rubbish. ...

By the process I have thus briefly sketched, the entire piers, excepting a small central portion, have been rebuilt from their foundations to their capitals; the new stone-work having to be inserted a little at a time, has been aided, in all cases, by strong copper cramps, so as to tie its courses together in their circuit round the pier.

All the stones are laid in strong cement, and all that remains within of the old work is run together at each course with liquid cement till it will hold no more. I saw, myself, ten pails full of this material poured into a single hole. ...

6

Celtic

Maen-du and Ynys Seiriol

Maen-du (dark stone) well in Brecon is neither a church nor a conventual building, and a date stone of 1754 accompanied an unspecified amount of renovation work. But it resembles the Oratory of Gallarus at Dingle, Co. Kerry, which dates from the sixth or seventh century, and gives a useful indication of the type of building that the Celtic monastery of Ynys Seiriol (Puffin Island) would have comprised. The Gallarus Oratory is perhaps the best example of a number of survivors in Ireland, and the style and method of construction indicate that the treatment of Maen-du as at least an authentic replica of a Celtic building is justified. Perhaps the most striking feature is the simple square-headed doorway with a single large lintel. No arch has been attempted, and the opening has a primitive functionality. The essentially dry-built walling has been contrived such that the roof rises to a point, and this forms a simple vault within. The curved roof profile has been achieved not by the use of voussoirs in compression in the manner of a conventional vault or arch, but by the technique of the impost or corbelled arch: a series of thin overlapping stones progressively reach across from each wall to form the pointed profile. A gable end is thus formed to the front and to the rear, and the shape of the roof consists of a multiplicity of tiny steps. A dry-stone wall can be a very durable structure as countless miles of walling enclosing farm and pasture land testify, and for dwellings it is easily made weatherproof by the application of plaster or daub.

Fig. 43 Brecon. Maen-du Well

The scant remains of the Celtic monastic settlement on Ynys Seiriol date probably from the seventh century, and the tower towards the centre of the enclosure or *llan* is a later twelfth century building associated with Penmon Priory just across the water. It is easy mentally to transpose Maen-du to this location in order to gain a good impression of what this Celtic monastery looked like, even though, as a recent visit revealed, the site is completely and densely overgrown.

Penmon

Penmon Priory's nave just across the water from Ynys Seiriol on Anglesey was built in the twelfth century, but the foundation seems to have remained Celtic until the adoption of the Augustinian Order early in the thirteenth century when a new presbytery and conventual buildings were added. The nave thus forms an important link with the Celtic past, and one would expect Celtic features. It is also worth noting that the Augustinian canons were closer in spirit to the Celts than were the other Orders with their less strict rule and greater involvement with lay society, and one can suppose that the transformation went relatively smoothly. But Penmon is a curious example of an ostensibly Celtic church. The nave and south transept, the west and south crossing arches, and the tower all date from the twelfth century, the north transept and presbytery being nineteenth-century rebuilds. The twelfth-century work is thoroughly Norman, and many similarities with small churches in England are seen.

It is a small, aisle-less cruciform church with a squat central tower. The nave has simple splayed windows, and there are north and south doors. There is no west door. The two original crossing arches are richly decorated in the Norman manner, and two of the south transept walls carry blind Romanesque arcading. The tower is a small, plain affair with pairs of round-headed windows in each face, the jamb shaft in the centre of each pair but none to either side contributing to the almost Saxon feel of these bell-openings. The squat pyramidal stone spire is typical of the Norman period, and it gives an indication of what was intended to surmount all towers, the spire executed either in stone as at Penmon and Ynys Seiriol, or in timber covered with lead or shingles. There are no obvious Celtic features in any of this, and some English churches of the period are similar in many ways. St Nicholas's Church at Old Shoreham in Sussex forms a good counterpart, and these two churches demonstrate how similar two examples of the architecture of Britain after the Norman Conquest could be, even when the buildings were

Fig. 44 Penmon. The font may have been made from the base of a high cross which was carved in about the year 1000

68

widely separated both geographically and politically. So on Anglesey, where Norman political influence was tenuous, we find a thoroughly Norman building which was apparently built for the Celtic church. Evidently its patron wished to demonstrate that he too could build on a scale and in a style which was prevalent in Norman-held territory, demonstrating his status as an equal.

It is only in the decoration of the south doorway that we see Celtic features. The

tympanum above the door (one of only two survivors in Wales, the other being at Llanbardarn Fawr, Aberystwyth) features a dragon in low relief, beneath which is a band of Celtic interlaced strap work. It was Celtic decoration rather than any architectural features which survived the Norman Conquest, but a possible exception is the Celtic-type square east end which was adopted in Britain generally during the twelfth century with the abandonment of the apsidal termination.

Fig. 45 Penmon. The tympanum above the south door

Fig. 46 Caldey. The gatehouse and the church tower

Caldey

Another island foundation is St Illtud's on Caldey which originally had a Celtic community. A Tironensian priory founded in 1131 as a daughter house of St Dogmael's, the buildings of St Illtud's date from the thirteenth and fourteenth centuries. It is very different indeed from Penmon, and although it was a Norman foundation of the Order of Tiron, the church and the remaining conventual buildings display both primitive construction and an almost total lack of dressed stone. The thirteenth-century church is a small, unaisled, two-cell structure consisting of a choir or presbytery with a sanctuary to the east. There is a western tower and spire of the Pembrokeshire type; that is, a relatively tall and slender tower without external buttressing, surmounted by a spire, these dating from the fourteenth century. They are the most overtly post-Conquest features. A very small cloister lies

Fig. 47 The prior's tower

Fig. 48 The sanctuary

Fig. 49 Looking south into the cloister

Fig. 50 The presbytery

to the north of the presbytery, and to the west of this there is a gatehouse with accommodation above. To the east of the cloister lies a two-storey building, a dorter occupying the upper floor, the kitchen and warming house the lower. North of the cloister lay the frater, now gone, and to the north-east lies the prior's tower, a rather substantial building which housed the prior's lodgings on the first floor. One gets the feeling that the standardized post-Conquest monastic plan was imposed upon a tiny foundation which could hardly accommodate it, and although the sanctuary of the church in particular belongs to the thirteenth-century Early English period with its pointed tunnel vault and the round moulded capitals supporting the arch of the east window, the atmosphere of this tiny church is quite unlike other post-Conquest examples on the mainland. It is therefore included in the present chapter where spiritually it would seem to belong, as it would find uneasy companionship with the likes of Brecon, Margam, and AbbeyCwmhir.

Newport

The Lady or St Mary's Chapel at St Woolos Cathedral in Newport occupies an unusual position to the west of the nave, the traditional place being east of the presbytery as one sees at St Davids and Llandaff. This is because St Mary's Chapel was built before the Normans came, and although it has been much altered it still contains pre-Conquest work in the lower sections of its walls. It is probable that the Normans decided to construct the present nave, complete with the elaborate west door which was surely not meant to be hidden away, with the intention of demolishing this existing church (it would have provided valuable working space if it was not still being used for worship) when the new work was finished. But for some reason it was retained, and it now finds itself sandwiched between the twelfth-century nave and the fifteenth-century tower. In about 1200 its walls were heightened and lancet windows were inserted, although the latter were altered in the nineteenth century. The tomb recesses along the walls also date from the Early English period. The square window in the south wall, believed to be an original opening, has been filled with octofoil cusping which came from the demolished fifteenth-century south porch. Finally, the outer walls have been refaced. Not much then remains visible of the Celtic structure, but it is a remarkable survivor nonetheless.

Fig. 51 Newport. South windows in St Mary's Chapel

Celtic decoration after the Normans:
Strata Florida, Conwy, Cymer, Valle Crucis, St Dogmaels

Figs. 53-54 Strata Florida. The west door, with details of the hood-mould stop and capital

In addition to the above-mentioned buildings there are a number of post-Conquest abbeys which demonstrate that the use of native-style decorative motifs persisted well into the thirteenth century. The northern half of Wales was not brought under the firm control of the English until Edward I's campaigns, and it was here where the Celtic decoration is mainly found. Also, it demonstrates how the original architectural austerity of the Cistercians, which went hand in hand with that Order's outlook, had been considerably relaxed by the end of the twelfth century. The carvings at Strata Florida and Valle Crucis are the most overt demonstrations of this, as the illustrations will show.

The Cistercian abbey of Strata Florida is an important example of a post-Conquest house which was endowed by the Welsh. It takes its name from an earlier foundation a couple of miles away which lay on the banks of the Afon Fflur, the River of Flowers. This earlier foundation dates from 1164, and it was endowed by Robert FitzStephen, a Norman baron who then held much land in this western part of Wales, but by the end of that year the Welsh uprising led by Rhys ap Gruffudd had begun, and it succeeded in expelling the Anglo-Normans from the area within two years. The present ruin is what remains of the abbey which was begun in 1184 under the patronage of Rhys, and the buildings were ready for occupation by 1203. Gruffudd endowed the monastery with properties, and his charter for the foundation was confirmed by Henry II. It was a staunch bastion of Welsh culture and heritage, and in 1212 King John felt uncomfortable enough with the situation to order its destruction, but this was never carried out.

Little remains of the monastery beyond the foundation walls, but the two striking features of what can still be seen are firstly the plan which follows the conventional Cistercian lines, and secondly the west door of the church which has remained almost complete. The Cistercians would of course have required a conventional layout, but the west door carries an extraordinary display of Celtic ornamentation superimposed as it were upon a late Norman form as an act of artistic and political defiance. This doorway features five continuous stepped roll-moulded orders, uninterrupted by capitals or separate jambs, and here we see the complete relaxation of emphatic Norman decoration in favour of the smooth, flowing lines which were to become the hallmark of the Early English style. Transverse straps of decoration are terminated by prominent triskels which proclaim the Celtic origins of the foundation around the monastery's most important doorway. Triskel swirls also adorned the crown of the arch and the labelstops, and such motifs can be found in Celtic art as far back as the early Iron Age in the first century, before the Romans came to Wales.

Fig. 55 Conwy. The west front

The present parish church within the city walls of Conwy was originally a Cistercian church, but much of it dates from after 1284 when the monks were forced to move from this strategically important site after Edward I's conquest. They were generously assisted by the king in establishing a new house a few miles down the valley at Maenan, but nothing of this remains above ground. At Conwy, the west door and the three lancet windows above are practically all that remain of the original church, but here as at Strata Florida we see a style of ornamentation around the door which is characteristic of the Celtic tradition rather than the stiff-leaf type which one would expect to find on a doorway dating from about 1200. Again, it is displayed on the important west door.

Fig. 56 Conwy. Capitals of the west door

*Fig. 57 Cymer. Only the nave of the church was built, in the early thirteenth century.
A west tower was added a hundred years later*

Cymer, a late Cistercian monastery dating from 1198, was founded by monks from Cwmhir under the patronage of Maredudd ap Cynan, cousin of Llywelyn the Great. The carvings on the capitals of the sedilia and the doorway to the west of it also show a marked Celtic influence, and a capital of the crypt at St Dogmael's Abbey is similarly adorned. But the most impressive collection of such capitals is to be found at Valle Crucis Abbey.

Fig. 58 Cymer. A capital of the sedilia

Fig. 59 St Dogmael's. A capital in the crypt

Valle Crucis is a Latin phrase which means the 'valley of the cross', and the abbey was so called because of its proximity to the ninth-century Celtic high cross, the Pillar of Eliseg, the remains of which stand a quarter of a mile to the north of the site. Another Cistercian abbey founded by a Welshman, Madoc ap Gruffydd Maelor, Valle Crucis was colonized by monks from Strata Marcella in 1201. Carvings on the capitals display a range of Celtic styles, and the collection of memorial slabs in the monks' dorter contains examples of the work of Welsh stone carvers who developed their own distinctive style of memo-

Figs. 60-66 Valle Crucis. Many capitals demonstrate the persistence of Celtic decoration in northern parts of Wales 150 years after the Normans came to Britain

Fig. 67 Valle Crucis. This tombstone, which dates from the early fourteenth century and is inscribed Maruruet, Daughter of (?), was used as a lintel above a fireplace when parts of the conventual buildings were converted into dwellings after the dissolution

Fig. 69 Valle Crucis. Thirteenth-century sculpture

Fig. 68 Valle Crucis. Tombstone of Madoc ap Gruffydd, d.1306

rial sculpture from the time of the Edwardian Conquest, having been introduced to it by the English earlier in the thirteenth century.

Examples of post-Conquest Celtic decoration can also be seen in numerous parochial churches in north Wales, and they illustrate the extent to which the Celtic spirit continued in this region compared with the Anglo-Norman dominated south.

Particularly at Valle Crucis, the early thirteenth century carving contrasts markedly with the stiff-leaf foliage which was ubiquitous in south Wales, and in Britain generally, at the time.

7

Norman-Romanesque

Chepstow

The priory church of St Mary at Chepstow contains some of the earliest surviving Norman work in Wales, and indeed in Britain. After the Norman Conquest, William FitzOsbern was granted the lordship of Striguil (Chepstow) as a reward for his successes in the campaign, and he began building there the earliest dated stone castle in Britain. It was usual for the Normans to found monasteries wherever they conquered, and the twin symbols of conquest — secular and religious — can be seen in many places where castle and abbey dominate the surrounding area, as at Chepstow itself, Usk, Abergavenny, Kidwelly, Pembroke, Monmouth, and Brecon. Ewenny had no castle in the near vicinity to protect it, and so it was surrounded by its own high walls, gate houses and turrets.

Chepstow Priory was a daughter house of the Benedictine abbey of Cormeilles in Normandy, and building began in about 1072. Since the dissolution the church has had a rather chequered history, but most of the original nave except for the aisles and the eastern (sixth) bay remains intact, and this part of the building dates from about 1100 or a few years earlier. A portion of the west front, built a little later in the twelfth century, also survives, but the western tower, transepts and chancel are modern. Despite the losses, St Mary's remains an impressive church, and the emphatic statement of a conqueror is still fully conveyed by this nave. It is a large building, and the elevations are divided into three: main arcade, gallery (or tribune), and clerestory. The approximate proportions are 2:1:1, that is the main arcades occupy fully half of the elevation with the gallery and clerestory sharing the upper half almost equally. The aisles are missing, and all of the arcades and galleries are walled up except for the easternmost bay on the south side, which alone gives an impression of the original design. The main arcade consists of very simple openings which convey the impression of being pierced through solid walls such that the piers are formed by the rectangular sections of walling in between.

The north gallery stage consists of single small plain openings positioned directly above the main arches, and they are about half the width of the clerestory windows above. The latter are also single plain openings, splayed in order to let in the maximum amount of light. The splay was an almost universally employed device during the Norman and Early English periods, and it allows a relatively small window opening (which would not always have been glazed) to let in light from many more angles than would a plain window tunnelled through a thick wall. Additionally, the splay itself, plastered white, reflects a good deal of light into the room. As window openings became larger during the thirteenth century the splay became almost redundant as a device for capturing light, assuming instead a rather more attenuated and decorative role.

The gallery stage on the south side is more elaborate, which suggests that it was built after the north side, changes of design as a building progressed being quite common. Here are found double openings with shafted jambs and cushion capitals, and there are pairs of shafts in the centre. The cushion capital, used a great deal by the Normans, consists of a block of stone with the lower sections of its corners chamfered towards a rounded profile at the base to form a smooth transition into the usually circular shaft which supports it. This produces a solid U-shaped pattern on each face. The gallery or tribune stage afforded an opportunity for architectural display without the need to consider glazing, and Chepstow offers an early example of the art. A roll-moulded string-course runs along the walls at the base of the galleries, and this and the dark gallery stage give a horizontal pull to the nave which relieves excessive verticality in such tall elevations. Missing are the engaged shafts which originally rose from the floor between each bay, probably to support a flat timber ceiling. There are no signs of a high vault having been built here, and the exterior walls again show no evidence of aisle vaulting. However, there has been much restoration at Chepstow, and Malcolm Thurlby (2006) has recently cited George Ormerod's 1838 report which described fragments of tufa vaulting in the nave. If the church was indeed given a high vault, it would make it one of the earliest examples in Britain — contemporary with Durham, for example.

The tooling on the stone is very coarse, this giving a good key or 'grip' for the plaster, and it is easy to forget that apart from the dressed stone forming the archways, columns and windows, the walls in this period were almost always intended to be plastered. This gave the buildings a much

Fig. 70 Chepstow. South elevation of the nave

Fig. 71 Lamphey. Flowers and false pointing lines painted on a window splay

brighter appearance than one often encounters today, and the large areas of walling provided space for the painter to display his art. Very few medieval wall paintings survive, but a good impression of what these buildings originally looked like can be gained from a visit to St Illtud's Church at Llanilltud Fawr (Llantwit Major) where very plain plastered arches can be seen in the presbytery between which are the remains of some paintings. Some thirteenth-century splays at the bishop's palace in Lamphey still show fragments of paint, showing the custom of applying false pointing lines to give the impression of walls built with well dressed stone. (This practice continues today.) As window openings increased in area and the art of stained glass emerged, the need to plaster interiors receded, and this was accompanied by improvements in the quality of masonry work so that smooth wall surfaces with narrow joints could be produced. Improvements in these areas after about 1100 can certainly be attributed to Saracenic influences with which western Europe came into contact during the First Crusade.

The west front at Chepstow displays fully developed emphatic Norman decoration. The doorway is decorated in six orders. The inner order takes the form of a plain roll-moulding, a continuous order uninterrupted by separate capitals or jambs being a favourite Norman device which is often seen alternated with shafted jambs. The inner orders feature triple chevrons (zig-zags), multiple diamond patterns, and multiple zig-zag patterns, and the last is another triple chevron. All of these orders except for the first are supported by capitals and shafts, and they are stepped to give an extremely rich effect with carefully graded patterns in both low and high relief.

The outer order particularly shows an unevenness in the sizes of the individual voussoirs, with consequent variations in the

Figs. 72-73 Chepstow. The west front and detail of the west doorway

79

dimensions of the sections of decoration, and this produces a rather wayward chevron which one sees in virtually all of the examples of the period. The arch was built up piece by piece around the centring with scant regard for the exact number of voussoirs needed to complete the arc, and at the crown one often sees stones of very different sizes employed to finish it off, contributing to the charm of these rumbustious creations.

The doorway is flanked by narrow blind arcades, and above there are three windows. These are of equal size, but the central one looks larger because it carries three orders of decoration. The two shallow clasping buttresses which flank the decorated west front carry newel stairs with narrow rectangular lights, and they are typical of the Norman period and a little beyond.

Llandaff

Little remains of the Norman cathedral at Llandaff, which was begun in about 1120 by bishop Urban, Llandaff's first Norman-appointed bishop. It had an unaisled nave, shallow transepts, and a presbytery which sported a highly decorated 'triumphal arch' at its eastern end which led to an apsidal sanctuary. This arch remains, together with sections of the original arches in the

Fig. 74 Llandaff. The sanctuary

south wall of the presbytery which have been cut through by later ones.

The great arch behind the high altar is a splendid example of mature Norman design, softer than Chepstow's west front, and richly decorated on its western side but not on the eastern side. This is because it led to the sanctuary, the principle being that a doorway or arch announced entry into a more holy place than the place that one was leaving. This can be seen everywhere. Nave doorways are decorated on their outsides but not on their insides (often to the detriment of the artistic effect of the nave's inner west wall). Chancel arches are decorated on their western faces but not on their eastern faces. And doorways connecting cloister walkways to naves and chapter houses are decorated on the cloister side rather than on the opposite side. Just occasionally, one can spot an oddity. For instance, the doorway high up in the south transept at Valle Crucis which led to the night stairs is decorated on the church side rather than on the dorter side, welcoming one into a dormitory full of sleeping Cistercians.

Fig. 75 Llandaff. The south door

Llandaff's great archway has four orders enclosed by a band of decorated roundels, and a cable-moulded string-course is applied to the wall at the point of springing of the arch, this continuing above the capitals to form a decorated abacus. Strictly an abacus is a separate thin plate of stone which sits between a capital and an arch, but one often sees it suggested decoratively as is the case here.

From about 1170 the original Norman building was updated. Aisles were added, and the late Norman north and south nave doors date from about this time. The south doorway has four very deeply stepped orders with large chevron patterns. Here is a good

Fig. 76 Llandaff. The north door

example of decoration applied both to the face and to the soffit of the arch such that the patterns meet at the edge to form a composite whole. The north doorway has three orders which make use of the same technique, and two of them are continuous. But here the hood mould carries a dogtooth decoration, a development of the square pyramidal nail-head which has had a V groove applied to each of its four sloping sides to form the characteristic cross shape in bold relief. It may well have become known as the dogtooth due to its slight resemblance to the dogtooth violet flower with its narrow swept back petals, but no-one is quite sure. It is most associated with the Early English style, and it replaced the chevron as the dominant decorative motif.

Ewenny

The church of Ewenny Priory existed before the Benedictine cell was established, but most of what can now be seen dates from after 1141, when it became a daughter house of Gloucester Abbey. It was never a rich house, and it had to spend considerable resources building containing walls and gatehouses, but this was fortuitous for us. Although the north transept, the transept chapels and the west front have been lost, the latter a cause for particular regret because comparisons with surviving west fronts at Chepstow and Margam would have been interesting, it remains a largely unaltered church which dates mainly from the mid twelfth century.

The north aisle was added to the nave when the church was adapted for monastic use. Today's aisle is a modern rebuild, the original aisle collapsing in 1803 just three years after the west range of buildings had been dismantled and cleared away. This clearance must have included a presumably dilapidated west front and the western-most bay of the nave. The massive plain drum piers, columns in their own right in contrast with the earlier work in Chepstow's nave, have round capitals which

Fig. 77 Ewenny. The nave arcade and clerestories   *Fig. 78 Ewenny. A crossing pier*

Fig. 79 Ewenny. South transept wall passage arcade

Fig. 80 Ewenny. A dragonhead labelstop in the north transept

carry light reeded patterns, but the arches are plain with square-moulded soffits. There is no gallery stage, the clerestories being simple splayed openings which are positioned above the piers of the main arcade rather than above the crowns of the arches. This creates a horizontal, syncopated rhythm, very different from the nave of Newport which will be looked at presently, and in Brecon's Decorated nave the same technique is used with similar results, avoiding excessive compartmentalization into separate vertical bays. At Chepstow this was avoided by the use of string-courses aided by the dark horizontal bands of the galleries.

The crossing arches at Ewenny have plain square-moulded profiles with similar soffits. The piers are robust square affairs, and the responds which support the arches rest upon high chevron-decorated steps. The south transept is lit by three impressive window openings in the south wall, one high up in the gable below the roof and two side by side underneath. The night stair is built into the south-west corner buttress, and this also communicates with a high wall passage built into the west wall which leads to the central tower, as at Brecon. Brecon's is lit by simple slit windows, but at Ewenny there is a lovely Romanesque arcade of seven bays with scalloped cushion capitals and a variety of round and square shafts. A delightful labelstop survives in the ruined north transept (Fig. 80).

Between the choir, which lay beneath the tower, and the presbytery stands a mid-fourteenth-century timber parclose screen with a central doorway. The unaisled presbytery is vaulted in two sub-divided bays; this is a tunnel vault with semi-circular arch ribs dividing it into four separate compartments, the alternating square and double roll mouldings of the ribs giving a pleasing effect. The sanctuary is of one bay with a ribbed, quadripartite vault. Double roll-moulded ribs have been used, and these are supported in the corners by scalloped capitals and responds which meet the string-courses. Only the sanctuary itself is lit, and this, the three steps up to it, and the more elaborate vault all emphasize its importance as the most sacred part of the church. The three windows in the east wall are graduated in both height and width, fore-runners of the classic Early English graduated lancets, and they are plain and splayed. Similar single openings are pierced in the north and south walls of the sanctuary. This well-lit part of the eastern arm contrasts strongly with the presbytery and the crossing area, and one should imagine what the original effect would have been like with the transept chapels lit by eastern lights. There was a strong lighting contrast between the altars and the rest of the space, and one sees similar arrangements at Llanthony and Valle Crucis for example. Even without its chapels and north transept, Ewenny has a delightful atmosphere, and the bright morning sun would have flooded the altars with light, invoking powerful spiritual sensations. The plain walling here was enlivened with paintings.

Tucked into the corner between the nave and south transept, two doorways gave access to the church from the cloister.

Fig. 81 Ewenny. The presbytery

Newport

A Robert de Hay controlled land in southern Gwynlwg as a fief from Robert fitzHamon, earl of Gloucester (Gwynlwg was a sub-kingdom that had been established on the west bank of the river Usk). Early in the twelfth century de Hay granted the church of St Woolos in Newport to Gloucester Abbey, and the latter provided funds for the building of the Norman work which can be seen today. It remained a parish church until it became the cathedral serving the diocese of Monmouth in the twentieth century.

The nave and west door of St Woolos date therefore from the early twelfth century and it is interesting to compare the nave with Ewenny's, the north arcade of which dates from a decade or two later. Newport's piers are again plain circular types which however manage to look rather slender, and the large square chamfered capitals are busily scalloped, this being a hallmark of the later Norman cushion capital. The arches are again plain with square soffit orders, and as at Ewenny this is rather austere for later Norman work. But the clerestories, unlike Ewenny's, are positioned above the crowns of the main arcade arches in the usual manner. There is a feeling of bay-by-bay verticality here, and again eastern clerestories have been altered at a later date to give more light to the Rood. The fifteenth-century aisles have been given roofs which meet the centre aisle walls above the clerestories so that they can give no light, and it is fortunate that the north aisle has large Perpendicular windows with plain glass to prevent an excessively dark interior. This nave is simple, pure later Norman work, and the open timber roof creates a useful sense of space within which these satisfying proportions can develop.

Figs. 82-83 Newport. The nave, looking west (top) and south

Figs. 84-85 Newport. The nave door and detail of the north capital

The west door which leads into the nave from St Mary's Chapel has an arch supported by detached shafts and capitals, the latter two believed to have come from the nearby Roman settlement of Caerleon. The leafy Roman composite capitals and tapering shafts are certainly unlike any Norman work of the period, and there is surely no reason to doubt that they are a Roman legacy. The capitals have been partly re-carved with crude figures, and the bases have roll-mouldings. The arch orders consist firstly of a simple chevron surmounted by a small roll-moulding, and then two projecting chevron orders are separated by a plain band. This is a simpler doorway than some of those already mentioned, but again the Norman use of bold patterns creates a remarkably rich effect with what is in fact an economy of means. The window above it with a splay on its eastern side suggests that demolition of the pre-Norman building to the west was indeed intended.

Penmon

The robust architecture of Ewenny and St Woolos, with its emphasis mainly upon plain regular mouldings, contrasts with the gentler roll-mouldings and circular shafting at Penmon which complement the rather more modest dimensions of this church very well, and these buildings demonstrate the adaptability of Norman design. The origins of Penmon Priory were discussed in the last chapter, and the church contains important Norman work dating from the middle decades of the twelfth century. It is a small cruciform church with a central tower, and remains of some of the conventual buildings which date from the thir-

Fig. 86 Penmon. The west crossing arch

Fig. 87 Penmon. The south crossing arch

teenth and sixteenth centuries lie to the south of the nineteenth-century eastern arm. The unaisled nave is lit by single high splayed windows in the north and south walls, which are not aligned with each other. A third, higher, splayed opening pierces the west wall. There is no west door, and the decorated south doorway was looked at in the previous chapter.

All of the crossing arches would have been decorated originally, but only the western and southern decorations survive. The former is splendidly decorated in two orders; chamfered imposts support the inner order, and beneath there are figured cushion capitals. The south one depicts a man with outstretched arms and legs as if falling, and the north one looks like a man bending to clutch a writhing staff, probably a depiction of Moses. The whole arch is enclosed by a triple-billeted hood-mould.

The south transept is lit by a splayed window in its east wall, and a higher opening in the south wall has been blocked by a post-medieval building. As with the arcading in the wall passage at Ewenny, one is delighted to find blind Romanesque arcading decorating the transept's south and west walls. There is an uneasy juxtaposition between the arcades in the corner, and one gets the feeling generally that the interior decoration was executed by masons who were rather less skilled than the master mason who designed it. It is quite possible that this wall arcading is not in its original position. There are many examples of doorways and arches being relocated in a building:

Fig. 88 Penmon. The south transept arcading

at Leominster Priory the complete thirteenth-century porch was dismantled and portions of it re-erected against the new fourteenth-century south aisle, and the most spectacular example in Wales is at Llanidloes, where the arcade and south doorway were brought from AbbeyCwmhir after the dissolution. At Penmon, the most important part of the original church was of course the chancel which contained the high altar, and the most elaborate decoration would have been seen here. Could it be then that when the Augustinians rebuilt the east end in the thirteenth century this arcading was removed from there and re-erected against the walls of the south transept? It would account for the fact that the arches in the south-west corner show no sign of having been designed to fit here, and also for the random ordering of the decorated shafts.

The whole of the interior is plastered, and shows well what was originally intended in these buildings. The small windows are assisted greatly by this, but of course the wall paintings have been lost.

Usk

The Benedictine priory for nuns at Usk was founded probably in the 1130s by Richard 'Strongbow' le Clare, and what a contrast there is between the handling of the Romanesque style here and at Penmon. The towers could hardly be more different in character, and at Usk we see a return to the plain angular mouldings of Ewenny and St Woolos. Originally, St Mary's was a small cruciform church without aisles, but a north aisle was added in the

Fig. 89 Usk. The tower

late twelfth century to give additional space for the parochial use of the nave. Since the dissolution the church has lost its transepts and presbytery, but the impressive crossing tower of the early twelfth century survives. It is divided into three stages, the lower being plain and rising just above the apex of the roof. The middle stage houses the bell-ringing platform, and the upper stage houses the bells. There is a later crenellated parapet. Simple string-courses separate the stages, and there is a large rotund stair turret built against the north-west corner. Few Norman towers have survived, and the one at Usk is starkly impressive.

The four crossing arches underneath are of comparatively modest dimensions, and the western arch, which unlike the other three is unsupported by blocking walls, is showing signs of depression brought about by the absence of transepts which formerly counteracted the outward thrust which the weight of the tower develops. This illustrates that there is little margin for error when a semi-circular arch is asked to support a great weight. A simple quadripartite vault is supported by scalloped capitals, and short shafts beneath them form inverted cones which quickly die into the walls. The eastern arch, which led into the presbytery and sanctuary, is more elaborate. Externally, there are signs of a tunnel vault which would have covered the eastern arm in the manner of Ewenny.

The crossing area is pure early twelfth-century Norman work, and although the scale is modest, the relatively plain decoration conveys an aesthetic strength.

Fig. 90 Usk. The crossing

Fig. 91 Usk. The north-east crossing capitals

Fig. 92 Margam. The nave

Fig. 93 Margam. The south nave aisle

Margam

Aesthetic strength can also be said to characterize Margam Abbey's nave. This Cistercian abbey was founded in 1147 by Robert Consul, Earl of Gloucester, as a daughter house of the French abbey of Clairvaux, which sent monks to establish the monastery. The buildings were completed by about 1180, but from about 1200 everything east of the nave was rebuilt in a sumptuous Early English style, and the ruins of this, the chapter house and associated portions of the eastern range show just how far the Cistercians had departed from their austere ideals. The nave continues in use as a parish church, one of only three Cistercian churches in Britain to do so, the others being Abbey Dore in Herefordshire (the transepts and eastern arm), and Holme Cultram in Cumbria, much of the nave here remaining. The remote sites of the Cistercian houses usually meant that their buildings fell into ruin after the dissolution, whereas many Benedictine churches continued in use: Brecon, Chepstow, Ewenny, Usk, Abergavenny, Monmouth, Kidwelly and Pembroke being a short list among many examples.

All but the eastern two bays of Margam's nave survive, with substantial portions of the west front. The aisles are modern, and the upper stages of the nave walls have been lost. Remains of blocked openings indicate that there was no gallery stage, and that the clerestory windows consisted of single tall openings, this being consistent with other Cistercian naves of the time. The immediate impression one gains from the surviving main arcades is that they are considerably earlier than their building date suggests. The arches are pierced through walls as at Chepstow to form crude rectangular piers, and square-moulded soffit orders continue to the ground which are punctuated by very small chamfered capitals which run around the piers in a decorative rather than a structural way. There are no nook-shafts in the corners, and if the original eastern part of the church looked anything like this, then it was an austere church indeed, very different from the work at Chepstow, Newport, and Penmon. The Cistercian ideal is fully conveyed here, and the almost complete, unaltered church ruin at Buildwas in Shropshire provides an excellent example of the sort of church that Margam must originally have been. The aisles have modern groined vaults which are authentic reproductions of Norman work up until 1100 or so, after which the ribbed vault came into vogue following that innovation at Durham Cathedral.

Those parts of the Norman west front which survive have an Italianate delicacy, far removed from the earlier Norman frontage of Chepstow and the doorways of Newport and Llandaff. The west door, the three windows above and the lower sections of the pilaster buttresses to each side are original, and the overall design similarity to the west front of Chepstow can be contrasted with the very different treatment of the decoration showing a generation of development between the two. The chevron teeth of the Conqueror have been drawn, and Margam's west door leads us towards the unbroken contours of the Early English style with its graceful roll-moulded orders. There are three detached shafts in each jamb, and each of these carry two very distinctive bulbous annulets, similar to the ones each side of the west doorway at Rochester Cathedral in Kent. Beneath delicately moulded abaci are graceful cushion capitals which feature a variety of foliated and non-figurative designs, and in the three windows above, continuous plain orders are followed by a

Fig. 94 Margam. The west front

Fig. 95 Margam. Capitals of the west door

91

series of rolls and hollow rolls, two detached shafts in each jamb again carrying bulbous annulets. Scalloped cushion capitals are crowned with abaci which continue as a string-course at the point of springing at the windows' heads, and a string-course at the base of the windows continues around the pilaster buttresses. A large inverted V groove over the doorway marks the position of a former canopy, and corbels can also be seen which supported the narthex, this having been a Cistercian church.

Benedictine naves were frequently used by the parish, and a selection of Norman fonts, typical of their time, is illustrated (Figs. 96-101). All of the Anglican cathedrals in Wales also serve as parish churches.

Figs. 96-101 Norman fonts. Top (left to right) Ewenny, Abergavenny, Newport
Bottom (left to right) Usk, Chepstow, Brecon

8

Transitional

Buildings which display characteristics that are both Norman and Early English can be termed Transitional, and the building date alone is an insufficient indicator. For example, Wells Cathedral, which was begun in about 1180, would not be described as anything other than Early English, whilst St Davids' nave, begun about 1182, is described as Transitional because it employs both rounded and pointed arches, and the decorations around the arches have affinities with both Norman and Early English work. Peterborough Abbey's nave was completed in 1193, entirely in the Romanesque style. It is very much a Norman nave.

Llanthony
The origins of the Augustinian priory of Llanthony were discussed in chapter one, but the ruins which one sees today date from building work begun after 1175, the canons having been forced to move to Gloucester, Llanthony Secunda, in 1136 because of Welsh hostilities during King Stephen's reign. But by 1175 a return was possible, and the church was built in a Transitional style. It is full of continuous ordered arches and window openings, and this gives it quite an individual character compared with other churches contemporary or otherwise. The master mason who designed it was obviously very much attracted to the technique, and the loss of much of this characterful church is a considerable cause for regret.

The west front is an ambitious affair, and this was the only monastic church in Wales to feature a pair of western towers (Fig. 102). The latter originally had four stages, but only three now remain. In the centre of the pair of blind lancets which decorate the third stages are triple engaged shafts with grooved, almost scalloped, trumpet bell capitals. This unusual form of capital, which also flanks the west window, can be seen in the contemporary crypt at St Dogmael's, and it is the main capital design used in other contemporary work at St Davids Cathedral. It has been fancifully known as the pollarded willow, and since it resembles nothing else there seems no reason why the delightful name should not be used. Above this triple capital there is a polygonal abacus, again strongly reminiscent of St Davids; such forms were used a great deal during the last quarter of the twelfth century, providing a strong punctuation to the flow between capital and arch. A painting by Edward Dayes (rear cover) of about 1800 shows that the west window consisted of three large graduated lancets decorated with dogtooth motif, and that the nave clerestory windows were tall, single, round-headed openings. Wall ribs also indicate that a stone vault was intended. Although old illustrations can be notoriously inaccurate in their detailing, this painter's accuracy with the other details which can still be seen today, and with the details seen in his other paintings, suggests that we can take this on trust. However, there are no signs of wall rib remains above the west crossing arch where a nave vault would have terminated, and this suggests that the nave may have been vaulted using wood.

The arches of the nave arcades are all similar except for the ones which comprise the easternmost bay, design changes in this area often being encountered. The pointed arches have three continuous orders, the central one being a small roll rather like a nook-shaft which continues right around the arch. The easternmost arches of each arcade have chamfered square orders instead of rolls, and fourth chamfered square soffit orders are supported by corbels with short shafts beneath. There is a roll-moulded string-course above the main arcade, this forming annulets to triple engaged vaulting shafts which interrupt it above each pier, and just below this the three shafts come together as inverted cones to die into the wall. The shafts have pollarded capitals and polygonal abaci, and the small blind-storey

Fig. 102 Llanthony. The west front

consisted of pairs of lancets with continuous orders, these rather like those at St Davids, although the latter has two pairs to each bay whereas Llanthony only had one. The clerestories are missing, and these were tall, single, round-headed openings. The chamfers which can be seen each side of the blind-storey lancet pairs rose to enclose them to form a unified design, again like St Davids. We saw at Chepstow that the tribune or blind-storey stage gave an opportunity for artistic display, and in England many good examples can be seen, for example at Lincoln, Durham, Romsey, Lichfield, Selby and Westminster Abbey. But in the Welsh churches it was generally either suppressed, as at Llanthony, or absent altogether, as at Brecon and Newport. It is true that there tends to be less emphasis upon height in the Welsh churches compared with their English counterparts which mitigates against a gallery stage, but it is absent even at Tintern, Neath and Llandaff, and these are all tall buildings.

The inner, soffit orders of the crossing arches are supported by triple engaged shafts, capitals and abaci which are to the same design as the nave's,

Fig. 104 Llanthony. A bay of the north nave arcade

Fig. 103 Llanthony. The nave

Fig. 105 (left) Llanthony. A crossing arch respond.
Fig. 106 (right) St Davids Cathedral. Transept vaulting shafts

but the middle shafts feature keel-mouldings (Fig. 105). Here the face of the shaft is drawn out to form a narrow pointed projection like the keel of a boat, and it is encountered from the late twelfth century onwards. Again, St Davids features it heavily (Fig. 106). The corbels which support these short engaged shafts have stiff-leaf foliation, stylized leafs based upon no particular species. These are also characteristic of the Early English period, and along with the dogtooth which was met with at Llandaff, the stiff-leaf dominated much late twelfth- and thirteenth-century decorative work.

The presbytery is of three bays divided by triple engaged vaulting shafts, the middle one again keeled. The eastern bay was the sanctuary, and it is the only one lit by window openings in the north and south walls as at Ewenny. These were very tall round-headed windows, and the south transept was lit by two similar windows pierced in the south wall surmounted by a central roundel. The crossing area supported a substantial tower.

The sacristy to the south of the south transept is vaulted in two bays, the ribs supported by pollarded willow corbels. Stiff-leaf bosses decorate the junctions of the ribs. It is a quadripartite vault, simply meaning that each bay is divided by two diagonal ribs which cross

Fig. 107 Llanthony. The crossing

over at the apex of the vault so as to form four compartments; the infilling between the ribs is called the webbing. From about the 1230s the vault would often carry a ridge rib running along the length of its apex parallel with the walls, and this was particularly favoured in Britain, whereas French masons tended to vault without a ridge rib. The sacristy's west doorway has shafted jambs and stiff-leaf capitals, and it led to the east walk of the cloister.

Llanthony's church was something of a trail-blazing design. Today, we see all manner of building styles from many eras, but we should try to imagine what Britain's architecture looked like in 1175 when the master mason began thinking about the design of the church for the newly returning Augustinian canons.

Everything looked Romanesque, and the illustrations of the previous chapter can be taken as a whole in order to try to gain an idea of how innovative the nave arcades of Llanthony would have seemed, together with the combined design of blind-storey and clerestory. Wells and Lincoln were just beginning, and St Davids' nave was about to contribute new stylistic innovations. This was an era unencumbered by mannered pastiches of style and reverence for the past. Margam knocked down its church's eastern end to build anew barely twenty years after it was completed. Tintern began a complete rebuild of its church a century after the original one was finished, and St Davids was rebuilt barely a generation after the building of the Norman cathedral. Llandaff demolished the north-western tower to build a Perpendicular one in the fifteenth century, leaving the Early English one on the opposite corner intact.

The Gothic era was a time of constant development and innovation, and although there were certainly influences from previous centuries emphasis was always upon the new. Only the twentieth century can be compared with the Gothic era in both the quality and the quantity of its original designs, and we are fortunate to live in an era which on the one hand builds the eastern end of Newport, the St David Chapel at Llandaff, Coventry, Liverpool and Guildford, but on the other hand forms such bodies as Cadw in order to preserve the great architecture of the past.

Usk

From the ruin of Llanthony we can now turn to the rather more modest arcading at Usk, which was erected in the late twelfth century when the nave was widened to accommodate the lay congregation. Untroubled by the presence of the existing Norman work, the master mason chose the pointed arch supported by round moulded capitals which are deeply undercut. The latter take the form of shallow inverted bells, and they anticipate the Early English undercut bell capitals of the transepts of Brecon, for instance, which were being built from about 1220. The plain round piers look back to the Norman era, but the easternmost has been decorated with four vertical roll-mouldings, this corresponding with the position of a screen which would have divided the parochial nave from the nun's church. This is all quite simple work with rough tooling, but already it demonstrates the value of the pointed arch in increasing the amount of light which a given span will allow. The height of the apex of the arch is greater than half of the span, and therefore the pointed

Fig. 108 Usk. The eastern pier of the nave arcade

profile gives an altogether lighter note than the Romanesque crossing arches. The latter suggest fortresses and castles as much as churches, whereas the former are always overtly ecclesiastical.

St Davids

In 1115 Bernard became the first Norman bishop of St Davids, and by 1131 he was able to perform a service of dedication in his new cathedral. Nothing of this building remains, for in about 1182 Bishop Peter de Leiâ began a complete rebuilding of the cathedral, unusually starting at the western end, only a generation after the Norman work would have been completed. It was customary to begin a rebuild at the east end of the church, usually to enlarge it to accommodate the increasingly elaborate processions and ceremonies, but de Leiâ chose first to replace the nave. This may have been because the original Norman building was structurally unsound, a problem which has afflicted the present one to a considerable degree. However, his nave constitutes the supreme example of Transitional architecture anywhere.

The nave is of six bays, the main arcades having round-headed arches except for the westernmost bay, which are pointed. Many examples of western bays which are narrower than those of the rest of the nave can be seen, and again the pointed arch demonstrates the freedom to vary the span-to-height ratio at will. The piers, massive affairs, are alternately round and octagonal, this often being encountered in Transitional work, and large engaged

Fig. 109 St Davids Cathedral. The nave, looking east

shafts decorate the cardinal points with pollarded willows forming the majority of the capitals (Fig. 110). Above, there are square protruding abaci, polygonal abaci crowning the capitals of triple engaged vaulting shafts in the aisles, these again being characteristic of late twelfth-century work. The square or polygonal abaci were seen at Llanthony, and Wells Cathedral and the choir of Canterbury have other

Fig. 110 St Davids Cathedral. Nave capitals

important examples of the period. These were soon abandoned in favour of circular abaci as one finds in St Hugh's choir at Lincoln which was being built from 1192, and the round profile certainly visually interrupts the flow between capital and arch a good deal less. The decoration of the arch orders is quite simple, being a combination of rolls and hollow rolls (the outer roll keel-moulded) except for the central orders, which continue the technique of combined face/soffit decoration which was seen in the north and south doorways of Llandaff for instance. A variety of patterns are employed including chevrons, lozenges, embryonic dogtooth and key patterns, and they are all in bold relief which creates a beautiful effect. The piers have round moulded bases which rest upon square plinths, the latter having projecting semi-octagonal platforms on the aisle sides which support the triple engaged vaulting shafts. The centre shafts are keeled, as are also the round bases beneath

Fig. 111 St Davids Cathedral.
Nave pier base, aisle side

to match, which is a nice touch (Fig. 111). The shafts are carried up such that their capitals are level with those of the piers, but similar shafts against the nave walls rise much higher. The original vaulting scheme, fragments of which can still be seen in the nave, either fell or had to be taken down when subsidence and a possible earthquake in the thirteenth century caused serious movement in the building, and the nave arcades can be seen to be leaning quite considerably.

The clerestory and blind-storey stages are markedly stepped back from the main arcades, and they have been combined into a single design which is indicated also at Llanthony. There are two bays here to each bay of the main arcade. The blind-storey is very simple, consisting of two lancets each with a continuous roll-moulding, and the spandrels have pierced splayed roundels which are elaborately decorated. Above is a round-headed clerestory window, which is splayed, and a continuous decorated face/soffit order encloses the clerestory which continues downwards to enclose the blind-storey too. Triple engaged vaulting shafts have centre keels and pollarded willow capitals with polygonal abaci, and they are aligned with the main arcade piers. Above the crowns of the main arcade arches there are single engaged shafts, and these all rise up as far as the base of the clerestory, after which timber shafts continue in order to support the magnificent early sixteenth-century roof of Irish oak. Its panels are enclosed by bands of complex open tracery work, and the carriage pendants convey a particularly Renaissance feel. The lovely colour of this oak harmonizes beautifully with the striking violet colour of the local sandstone. String-courses above the main arcades draw the eye towards the nave altar and Alban Caröe's twentieth-century rood and bishop Gower's sumptuous Decorated pulpitum, features that will be examined in a later chapter.

Fig. 112 St Davids Cathedral. The nave, looking west

The west wall of the nave belongs to Scott's nineteenth-century restoration, as indeed does the west front, and apparently he was following what was known of the original design from a drawing found in the library of the Society of Antiquities, made before it was superseded by a design of John Nash in 1793. The doorway, the three windows above and the five graduated clerestory windows all carry round heads, the latter group being enclosed by a large face/soffit-decorated arch. The windows do not align with any of the arcades of the nave's elevations, and the west wall gives the impression of halting the nave in mid flow; the pointed arches at this end of the nave contribute to the squashed up effect.

But the design of the nave of St Davids is a brilliant success. Although the piers are massive and the arches of the main arcade are boldly Romanesque, the whole composition is lightened by the incisive and inventive decoration which breaks up the lines and fascinates the eye. It seems timeless. It feels nothing like earlier naves at Newport, Chepstow and Margam, and nor does it feel anything like the work which immediately followed at Llandaff and Brecon. Even contemporary Llanthony is very different despite numerous similarities of detail.

St Davids' presbytery shares many of the nave's features, but it is a rather less successful design, due no doubt to some serious interruptions. The central tower collapsed eastwards in 1220 bringing down with it three of the crossing arches and the upper stages of the eastern arm. The original western crossing arch is round, the rest are pointed. There is a great deal of Scott's restoration work in the crossing area where the choir is situated, but he was faithful to the original design.

Fig. 113 *St Davids Cathedral. Detail of the nave roof*

After the tower's collapse the upper walls were repaired — the break in the masonry can be clearly seen immediately above the clerestories — and the presbytery as we see it today was completed somewhat later in the thirteenth century after an earthquake caused further damage. It is of four bays, and again the piers alternate between circular and octagonal, the latter being irregular. But gone are the large engaged shafts at the cardinal points, and this exposes the cores to create a ponderous effect. The pointed arches compose with them much less successfully than do the nave's rounded ones, but the narrower bays required them in order to develop the necessary height. The juxtaposition between capital and arch is uneasy; the arch merely sits on top whereas in the nave it seems to develop naturally. The carving around the capitals is here uninter-

Fig. 114 *St Davids Cathedral. The presbytery, with the fifteenth-century timber sedilia*

Fig. 115 St Davids Cathedral. The presbytery's east lancets

rupted by shafts, and it is a little fussy. The triple vaulting shafts against the piers rise up to cut through the outer orders of the arches which creates a pinched effect. There is no blind-storey, but the tall splayed hood-moulded clerestory lancets, with continuous keel-mouldings and face/soffit decorations, are pleasing. The vaulting shafts are crowned with capitals and polygonal abaci just below the string-course at the base of the clerestories, and they leave the sections of walling above awkwardly blank, this only partly mitigated by some niches which were inserted later in the thirteenth century on the north side.

The clerestory lancets in the east wall belong to Scott's restoration after he took out a very squat Perpendicular window, and these are richly moulded and shafted in an Early English manner which however does not match the other work in the presbytery. But the three large eastern lancets, survivors from the first stage of the rebuilding of the east end, are magnificent. They are only just pointed, recalling similar groupings at Wells and Salisbury, and their splays are replete with the Transitional motifs which one finds in the nave. Hood-moulds with carved labelstops enclose the lancets, and the splays are terminated with keel-moulded shafts which are decorated with a series of annulets. Limestone has been alternated with sandstone in the upper sections of the decoration which further enhances the beautiful effect, and beneath there is a key-patterned string-course upon a band of interlocking Romanesque arcading. The lancets, which formerly looked into the retro-choir, were blocked in the early sixteenth century when Bishop Vaughan built the Holy Trinity Chapel, and they are now decorated with Salviati's nineteenth-century mosaics.

St Davids church was an ambitious design, intended to reflect the status of the diocese and its bishop. The decoration in the nave especially is of a very high order, and the overall design shows an awareness of prestigious building work going on elsewhere at the time, for instance at Canterbury, Wells, and Glastonbury. Most strikingly, and now not readily apparent as the design is not fully implemented because of trouble with the foundations, was the projected vaulting scheme. The alternating triple and single engaged shafts above the main arcades imply a sexpartite or 'ploughshare' vault, the triple shafts receiving three vault ribs, a transverse rib flanked by diagonal ribs. The single engaged shafts were to receive simpler transverse ribs. This kind of vault was in favour during the years around 1200

Fig. 116 St. Davids. Porth y Tŵr. This detached bell tower, or campanile, was built on the hill next to the cathedral in the thirteenth century

and can be seen above the choir at Canterbury and in Lincoln's transepts, as well as in French buildings of the time. Daringly, at St Davids a tall wall passage runs along the length of the nave behind the combined blind-storey/clerestory stage, this leaving an open space immediately behind the wall against which the vault would have abutted. With this in place, it would have created the visual effect of the vault sailing above the nave, lit by the clerestory windows, with little to support it. In fact the main support would have been the sections of walling between the clerestories, the substantial parapet seen on the exterior of the building adding considerable 'mass loading' to support and stabilize the whole design. Clearly, the designer of this nave was of the first rank. The robust, Romanesque main arcade however looks backwards, and must have been chosen for ascetic reasons. Perhaps there was a desire to reflect aspects of the building which it replaced.

In the thirteenth century a detached bell tower was built to the south of the cathedral. Evidently the weight and stresses caused by a full peal of bells were not to be risked in the new tower of the church following the structural problems that it had suffered.

St Dogmael's

The last building to be looked at in this chapter is the crypt of St Dogmael's Abbey; there are strong stylistic links with contemporary work at St Davids. Numerous crypts survive in England, dating mainly from Norman and even Saxon times. Ripon's crypt dates from about 675. Early Norman cathedrals in England usually had east ends which were built

Fig. 117 St Dogmael's. The crypt

on a higher level than the naves with crypts underneath such as at Winchester, Rochester, Gloucester (then an abbey), Canterbury and York. They can be lovely secretive chambers: the word derives from the German *kryptien*: to hide; and Worcester's example which dates from the 1080s demands special mention. They were intended at least in part to house the remains of holy relics, and one can picture processions of pilgrims filing down the stairways in the hope of finding spiritual enlightenment or the return to good health. But crypts fell out of fashion during the twelfth century as shrines were moved from underground to be displayed in the main body of the church, and Wales never favoured them at all; it is therefore surprising to come across one at the Tironensian abbey of St Dogmael's, built in about 1200. The original Norman church here probably suffered damage during the latter part of the twelfth century when the Lord Rhys was driving out the Anglo-Normans in south-west Wales, and rebuilding became necessary. The remains of the apsidal chapel in the south transept suggest that the original church could also have had an apsidal presbytery or sanctuary which projected a comparatively short distance east of the crossing, as was the case at Llandaff, the Norman archway of which remains. Rebuilding included the oft-encountered eastward extension, but here the site of St Dogmael's slopes rapidly away, and one suspects that this provided the incentive to indulge in a crypt over which the presbytery could be built.

The crypt has a square plan and was vaulted in four compartments with a central pier. Access was provided by a stairway built into the thickness of the wall in the north-west corner which would have made it secretive indeed, and it was lit by openings in both bays to the east and to the south, the north face having a window in the eastern bay with the stairway to the west. Triple engaged vaulting shafts, the middle one keel-moulded, were placed in the centre of each wall. There were bases to match, and the capitals were pollarded willows. Single keeled engaged shafts were placed in the corners. All this is very like contemporary work at St Davids and Llanthony, and it suggests that a master mason with rather individual ideas was active in southern parts of Wales during the decades either side of 1200, inspiring some notable Transitional creations. But here the keel-moulding, instead of being pointed, has a flat face so that it forms a shallow rectangular strip on the face of the shaft. It was introduced very shortly before 1200, and Brecon's presbytery, which was being rebuilt from about this date, also employs it.

9

Early English

Llandaff

We are lucky that Llandaff Cathedral exists at all. It has been rescued from the brink of destruction on more than one occasion, and during the course of its history it has suffered greatly from both wanton damage and neglect. The building which one sees today is the result of considerable restoration work in the nineteenth and twentieth centuries, but the restorers managed to rescue the medieval character of this great cathedral whilst also making some notable contributions of their own.

Bishop Urban's cathedral was begun in about 1120, and in about 1170 the outer walls of the nave and the north and south doors were built. Then came the rebuilding of the four eastern bays of the nave in the Early English style. The arches of the bay immediately to the west of the presbytery have sub-arch infillings which strengthened them in preparation for a central tower over a crossing area, which was however never built. The same technique was employed at Glastonbury Abbey at about the same time. One also notices considerable design similarities in the nave piers of Llandaff and the crossing piers of Glastonbury, very different from the near-contemporary work of Wells only a few miles to the north of Glastonbury. After a pause, the western four bays of the nave were built beginning in about 1200, and the west front followed in about 1220. The eastern and western bays of the nave show the usual changes in design details: the arch-mouldings are different, triple engaged shafts took the place of sunken shafts, and the semi-arches supporting the nave walls in the aisles gave way to complete transverse arches further west. Finally, the arches of the two bays which comprise the

Fig. 118 Llandaff. The nave, looking north-east

*Fig. 119 Llandaff. The nave,
looking south-west*

Fig. 120 Llandaff. The chapter house

presbytery and the sanctuary were cut through Urban's original Norman work, remains of which can still be seen on the south side. The capitals of the engaged shafts of this later work are rounded in contrast to the nave's earlier semi-polygonal ones. The chapter house was built to the south of the presbytery in about 1250, and then followed the Lady Chapel during the latter half of the thirteenth century, which occupies the usual position as an eastward extension. Heavily restored, it nevertheless displays the characteristic features of the early Decorated period with its geometric bar tracery. Its east window belongs to the nineteenth century, and it is a successful and appropriate design.

To the first half of the fourteenth century belong the nave and presbytery aisle windows and the upper sections of the eastern arm with its exterior Decorated parapet, and the fifteenth century saw the erection of the north-west 'Jasper' tower, named after its benefactor Jasper Tudor, Duke of Bedford and uncle of Henry VII. All this ongoing work was typical of the medieval period, and it created an impressive cathedral which could boast excellent examples of all of the architectural styles. But after the religious turmoil of Henry VIII's reign the fabric began to fall into neglect. Bishop Blethin, appointed in 1575, did much to raise funds to carry out essential repairs, but he had to decrease the personnel, disband the choir, sacrifice the choral services, and dispose of the organ in order to do so. But the problems were hardly arrested, and in 1697 Archdeacon Bull described Llandaff as a 'sad and miserable cathedral'. Cromwell's troops had earlier turned the nave into a beer house and a post office, and they burnt all of the chapter library books. In 1703, a storm removed the parapet of the Jasper tower, and the thirteenth-century south-west tower was destroyed in another storm twenty years later, bringing down with it the nave roof. The final indignity came when John Wood the elder, famous for his eighteenth-century Georgian work at Bath, erected his 'Italian Temple' amid the ruins of the nave with the intention of creating an appropriately fashionable Picturesque setting for his work. Fortunately, the money ran out, and further destruction of the cathedral ruin was avoided.

The Gothic Revival movement of the nineteenth century stimulated an interest in and respect for medieval architecture, and Llandaff benefited from this. Wood's temple was pulled down, the Lady Chapel and the nave were restored, and a service of thanksgiving was conducted in 1869. John Prichard was the architect in charge, and he was responsible for the design of the south-west tower and spire and the chapter house roof. He was also responsible for the row of sovereigns' heads which adorn the corbel table of the nave's south aisle roof, and these continue on the north side. Restoration was completed, a new organ was installed, and choir services were again heard.

Then, in 1941, a German bomb exploded immediately to the south of the nave. Among Britain's cathedrals, only that of Coventry suffered greater damage during the Second World War. It blew in the nave and chapter house roofs and the tracery of the south aisle windows, and the nave was filled with rubble. Prichard's spire was rendered unsafe, and the organ and furnishings were destroyed. The Norman south doorway miraculously survived. Sir Charles Nicholson was placed in charge of the post-war restoration, and on his death in 1949 George Pace took over. Pace built the Welsh Regiment (St David) Chapel to the north of the nave, and also the parabolic arch of reinforced concrete in the nave which forms the great Rood. A

Fig. 121 Llandaff. The choir and presbytery

Fig. 122 Llandaff. Early English stiff-leaf foliage on the south presbytery doorway

Fig. 123 Llandaff. George Pace's Welsh Regiment (St David) Chapel

Fig. 124 Llandaff. Sir Jacob Epstein's Majestas

cylindrical chamber which is supported by the arch houses the positive organ, and sixty-four gilded pre-Raphaelite figures which formerly decorated the pre-war choir stalls adorn it. On the western face of the cylinder is Sir Jacob Epstein's Majestas which was cast in unpolished aluminium at the Morris Singer Works in Lambeth.

The Early English nave of Llandaff has no gallery or tribune stage, and the tall clerestory is a nineteenth-century rebuild which is believed to have been faithful to the original design. The main arcade arches consist of continuous chamfered orders, the soffit-orders supported by semi-octagonal abaci upon stiff-leaf capitals. The triple engaged shafts beneath all carry keel-mouldings, here drawn outwards to form a simple point which in section resembles a plain pointed arch, different from the keel-mouldings of Llanthony and St Davids, which in section form an ogee profile: a stretched out S curve leaning towards the left against a mirror image of itself. Moulding profiles would have been drawn by the master mason to which his masons would work, and therefore the ogee form was regularly before his eyes as early as the twelfth century. But it wasn't until the 1290s that the ogee began to be used in Britain as an arch or canopy profile, the first known usage being in the design of Edward I's Eleanor Crosses, which were erected to mark the resting places of his queen's body as it was transported southward for her funeral in Westminster Abbey. Thereafter, the ogee became ubiquitous in window tracery and other decorative work throughout the medieval period, and Llandaff's nave aisle windows are impressive examples. But the ogee was not favoured as an arch profile if any significant weight was to be borne, because the apex represents a point of structural weakness: the two major curves of the arch do not lean directly against each other.

In contrast with the west bays, the three easternmost shafts which rise from the springing of

Fig. 125 Llandaff. The 'Trinity' corbel in the south nave aisle. Three heads share four eyes

the arches are single keel-moulded types which are sunken into grooves. They punctuate the bays much less than do the triple ones, and these eastern bays have a considerably more horizontal pull as a result. The later piers have vertical V-grooves along their diagonals, and the arches of the westernmost bay carry an extra moulded order.

Figs. 126-127 Llandaff. Nave pier, capitals and base

The slightly stepped back clerestory consists of pairs of tall lancets in each bay, flanked and separated by narrow blind lancets. Detached shafts support the heads of the latter, and they have round moulded bases and stiff-leaf capitals. This attractive clerestory is a nice example of the use of lancets of equal height. Later they tended to be graduated in height and often in width too, but Llandaff's impart a continuous horizontal rhythm here which complements the verticality of the tall main arcade.

To the south of the presbytery lies the chapter house, a square vaulted chamber of the mid-thirteenth century. Modern additions include George Pace's Welsh Regiment (St David) Chapel and Alan Durst's font. A medieval corbel looks on. Details of the nave piers, very similar to contemporary work at Glastonbury, are shown.

Fig. 128 (left) Llandaff. The modern font, carved by Alan Durst. The carvings depict Man's Fall, Christ's Redemption, and scenes from the lives of saints Dyfrig and Teilo

109

Figs. 129-130 Llandaff. The west front and the Prichard tower (right)

The modern Rood which spans the nave will of course continue to provoke discussion. It never looks convincing in illustrations, but one's opinion should not be based upon these. To see it in real life is a different experience altogether, and a memorable one.

The west front dates from a decade or two after Llanthony's, and the loss of Llandaff's original western towers makes comparisons difficult. But the tall, simple lancets, punctuated by narrow blind ones which recall the clerestory, impart an aesthetically pure feeling which is characteristic of Early English work, in some ways a rebellion against the emphatic broken-up decoration of the Normans. Pairs of western towers which do not match are unusual in Britain, but there are plenty of Continental precedents. Prichard's nineteenth-century tower and spire were designed to blend in with the Early English work, and although his parapet and spire are rather elaborate for the early thirteenth century the whole is a very pleasing design which is much more successful than a lot of other nineteenth-century Gothic.

Brecon

The Early English nave of Llandaff stylistically resembles work at Glastonbury, and it can be linked to a particular regional 'school', but the work which immediately followed at Brecon belongs to no such school. The design of the presbytery is very much a one-off, and it is outstanding. Brecon Cathedral began life as a Benedictine priory, a daughter house of Battle Abbey in Sussex. It was founded by Bernard of Neufmarché probably a little before 1100, and it is not clear whether there was already an existing church on the site. The only substantial remains of a Norman church are the large areas of blank walling immediately to the west of the crossing space which forms the eastern bay of the nave. Rebuilding began soon after 1200 under the patronage of William de Breos, Lord of Brycheiniog, starting at the east end as was usual. The presbytery dates from the first quarter of the thirteenth century, after which there was a pause brought about by de Breos's fall from royal favour: King John was claiming payments from his estates which were overdue. De Breos fled to exile

Fig. 131 Brecon Cathedral. The presbytery

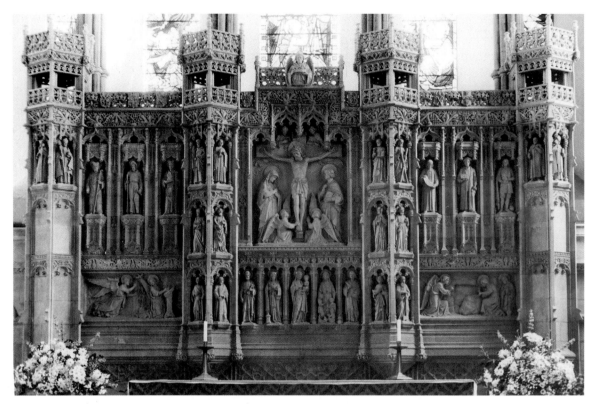

Fig. 132 Brecon Cathedral. The reredos

in Ireland, after which he aligned himself with Llywelyn the Great. The cathedral's transepts date from around the second quarter of the thirteenth century, and thus two distinct phases of the Early English style are seen at Brecon which are fascinating to compare. The presbytery is a wonderful design, beautifully refined, and the masonry shows a very high standard of tooling. The transepts are altogether more robust, the mouldings are simpler and more emphatic, and the tooling is coarser. Fortunately, the slender lancet groupings of the presbytery are echoed in the north and south walls of the transepts, and these are all very beautiful.

The east window consists of five graduated lancets which virtually fill the wall space. The central three are pronouncedly stilted, rising high above the capitals and clusters of shafts which support them before the lines are allowed to converge. Their multiple roll-mouldings grow out of the shafts with an easy flow which has not hitherto been achieved, and the moulded bell capitals have been sensibly chosen in preference to stiff-leaf foliage which would have broken up the composition too much. Moulded annulets in the centres of the shafts punctuate the design, and the round moulded bases rest upon a string-course which runs around the whole of the presbytery, dividing it up into areas of walling and fenestration. The deep splays and the walls are here plastered white, just as they should be, and the lighting is delicious. The north and south walls carry three bays of extraordinary graduated lancet triplets, immensely tall and slender, again stilted to further emphasize verticality with clusters of shafts and rich vertical arch mouldings. Gone are the square or polygonal abaci of the earlier work of the period, and all is smooth, clean and chaste. Further clusters of shafts rise from moulded round corbels to support the vaulting, the central one detached; never implemented at the time (the slightly uneasy juxtaposition of shaft and neighbouring arch suggesting that the vault may have been an afterthought anyway), the vault dates from Scott's nineteenth-century restoration. A simple quadripartite vault in four bays, it is without a ridge rib in the French manner, the arch ribs delicately moulded so that nothing here disturbs the beautifully smooth lines. It is very much in line with what was originally intended, and if, strictly speaking, the vault webbing would have been plastered white to assist in the lighting of the space, the presbytery is so well lit anyway that the colour of natural stone above our heads is not unwelcome.

The triple sedilia has roll-moulded cusped heads which are supported by detached shafts, and the unusual triple piscina complements the design. Again, this is Early English work of the highest order, and one wonders what the monks thought of the great contrast between the new work and their old Norman nave.

The stone reredos is modern, and it was designed by W.D. Caröe. The style is late medieval, and is a typical example of the care with which this architect treated ancient buildings in his role as Architect to the Ecclesiastical Commissioners. He died in 1938, and his business was continued by his son Alban, who among other things designed Newport's east end and the rood and organ case of St Davids. His son Martin continues the dynasty, and the family has been notable for a level of taste and understanding which was often lacking in the Victorians.

The doorways which lead from Brecon's presbytery to the transept chapels belong to the second building phase, and they immediately strike a different note with their robust angular orders. There are four jamb shafts in addition to the engaged shafts which support a soffit order, and here the bell capitals have been very deeply undercut, a feature in all of the capitals of this later work. The crossing arches have large chamfered square orders which are supported by bell capitals and engaged shafts, the latter carrying keel-mouldings of the type also encountered in the crypt of St Dogmael's. Here, the keel is not pointed but flat: it is a shallow rectangular strip which joins the shaft with only a slight curve. It also decorates the arch mouldings and the string-course of the presbytery, but the shafts were very sensibly left plain.

Fig. 133 Brecon Cathedral. Deeply undercut capitals in the north presbytery doorway

*Fig. 134 Brecon Cathedral.
The east end*

The exterior of Brecon Cathedral is plain and fortress-like. The lancets in the eastern arm look incredibly thin, mere slits in the walls, and they betray no hint of the sumptuous work inside. The upper stage of the tower dates from about 1300 with Perpendicular reworking, but one would hardly call it 'decorated'. The eastern corner buttresses are capped with delightful spirelets which belong to Scott's restoration, the octagonal spires being surrounded by further miniature spires at their diagonals. The stepped buttresses are decorated with bands of moulding, and this eastern face of the cathedral provides the chief external interest along with the attractive north face of the nave.

Margam

The rebuilding work at the east end of Benedictine Brecon constituted the initial phase which was to continue with the renewal of the entire church, and one smiles when one sees the ruins to the east of Cistercian Margam Abbey's nave. From about 1200 the monks built themselves lavish new surroundings, but left the lay-brothers' nave untouched. Here at Margam there is yet another interpretation of Early English work as compared with that at Llandaff and Brecon, and it has affinities with contemporary work at Abbey Dore and Wells. The ruins include substantial remains of the chapter house and its entrance vestibule, with parts of the eastern section of the church. There are also some remains of conventual buildings to the south.

The chapter house is entered via a large vestibule with smaller side aisles, all vaulted in two bays. The vaulting ribs die into piers to form continuous smooth lines down to the

*Fig. 135 Margam. The chapter house
entrance vestibule*

Figs. 137-138 Margam.
Chapter house vaulting corbels

Fig. 136 Margam. Chapter house vestibule vaulting corbel

ground, and in the corners they are supported by corbels. The vestibule's entrance doorway carries many roll-moulded orders, keels again in evidence, and a central dogtooth order adds further interest. The jambs each carry three nook-shafts with keel-mouldings and annulets, and they stand upon round bases. This doorway is in general form rather similar to the west door of the church, which dates from a generation earlier. The capitals are of a design which has not fully relinquished Norman influence, and one is quite surprised to see these among all this Early English work.

As grand as many a chapter house itself, this vestibule leads to Margam's large rotund chapter house proper, which is twelve-sided without. Large single lancets pierce each face, each featuring a continuous chamfered order surmounted by another which is supported by nook-shafts with moulded round bases and annulets. The capitals carry square abaci, and they are decorated with motifs some of which look back towards later Norman work, and others which are stiff-leaf. The eastern lancet carries roll-mouldings on its outer order, distinguishing it as the bay where the abbot would sit to preside over the daily chapter and, unusually, the internal decoration of the lancets is exactly duplicated on the outside of the building except for the extra mouldings of the abbot's bay.

Fig. 139 Margam. The chapter house

The central pier consists of a cluster of shafts, and this cluster is supported by a base which complements the profile. It rests upon a circular plinth. The capitals carry stiff-leaf foliation, and again the abaci echo the profiles of the shafts beneath. Twenty-four vaulting ribs sprang from this pier, but one must go to

Fig. 140 Margam.
The south transept window

the chapter house of Lincoln Cathedral to appreciate what has been lost. This Early English work, contemporary with Brecon's presbytery, shows just how different could be the conception of the style in the minds of two master masons: the work at Margam is bold, robust, and full of a strength which develops earlier Norman repose, whereas at Brecon we sense rather more forward-looking thinking as an emphasis upon mass and strength is relinquished for a more ethereal outlook.

The transepts and presbytery of Margam's church feature window openings which consist of pairs of lancets surmounted by quatrefoil plate tracery. The quatrefoil is pierced through solid walling, the principle as applied to the blind-storey of St Davids' nave. At Margam it is employed as a window opening, and it shows how the space above and between a pair of lancets came to be utilized as an additional source of light. Plate tracery of this type can also be seen in Tintern's frater, the west front of Valle Crucis, and in the chamber south of the eastern slype at Neath. It is surprising how much more light this extra piercing lets in, and particularly at Valle Crucis one sees that bar tracery is virtually inventing itself before one's eyes.

Neath

In contrast with Tintern, so much of the dressed stone at Neath has been robbed out that architectural details are scarce. This is a particular source of regret because the church was rebuilt between 1280 and 1330, a decade or two later than Tintern's, and the two Decorated churches would have been very interesting to compare. Neath's conventual buildings to the south-east were also subject to much post-dissolution alteration when they were converted into a Tudor mansion. The most impressive chamber remaining is the early thirteenth-century undercroft beneath the monks' dorter, two bays by five, which has a quadripartite vault without ridge ribs. The plain, slim cylindrical piers with their moulded round bases and capitals recall later Norman work, but the corbels which support the vault around the walls are of the moulded bell type, beneath which are short shafts, and these form cones which die into the walls. This is a large and impressive undercroft, the bold chamfered vaulting ribs supported by the slender piers demonstrating the increasing appreciation of the balancing of thrusts and counterthrusts as the piers are asked to support only the dead weight of the vault. Clasping buttresses on the wall exteriors visually counteract the outward thrusts, but in truth the upper walls with their mass loading do most of the stabilizing work. Unfortunately the fenestration is not original, and one would presume single lancets here when first built.

Neath

Figs. 141-142 (right) Plate tracery and doorway south of the eastern parlour

Fig. 143 (below) Monks' dorter undercroft

Fig. 144 Llanidloes. The nave arcade was brought from AbbeyCwmhir after the dissolution

Fig. 145-146 Llanidloes. Details of the nave arcade

AbbeyCwmhir

Moving on a decade or two brings us to the remains of AbbeyCwmhir with its fully mature Early English nave. The chief attraction of this Cistercian monastery (the Abbey of the Long Valley) is its magnificent setting. Not much of any architectural interest can now be seen, but in its prime it must have been one of the most impressive buildings of its age. The circumstances of its original foundation are obscure, but it seems to have been re-founded at its present site in 1176 by Cadwallon ap Madog, Lord of Maelienydd, who was cousin of Rhys ap Gruffydd, prince of south Wales, and re-founder of Strata Florida Abbey. The abbey spent its life performing a delicate balancing act between loyalty to the Welsh rulers and loyalty to the English crown, and this Cistercian house therefore bridged a gap geographically between the Anglo-Norman foundations to the south — Neath for instance having originally been a Savignac abbey founded in 1130 by Richard de Granville — and the Welsh Cistercian houses in the north such as Strata Florida, Valle Crucis, and Cymer.

In 1214 King John took the abbey under his protection, but in 1231 during the war between Henry III and Prince Llywelyn ab Iorwerth (the Great) the monks deliberately misdirected

118

the king's forces which led to their defeat. The king plundered one of the abbey's granges in revenge, and the abbey itself was saved only because the payment of a fine of three hundred marks was made. Llywelyn ap Gruffydd (Llywelyn the Last) was supported by the abbot of Cwmhir during the wars with Edward I, and when he met his end in 1282 near Builth it is believed that Llywelyn was buried at the abbey. A modern inscribed tombstone has recently been placed in the nave ruin to commemorate him.

The ruins date from the early thirteenth century, and the 242-foot nave was the largest in Wales. Obviously the church was planned on a lavish scale, but in the event only the aisled nave of fourteen bays and the west walls of the transepts were built. Cymer, which was colonized by monks from Cwmhir in 1198, also managed to complete only the nave of its church, and both were unusual therefore in that it was the nave which was the first part of the church to be built, whereas it was customary to begin building at the eastern end. Soon after the dissolution, the parish church of Llanidloes about ten miles to the north-west was being extended, and six complete arches were removed from the abbey to be re-erected in St Idloes. They stand there today, five forming the arcade between the nave and the north aisle, one forming the south door, and the quality of their design and execution indicates that Cwmhir must have been quite a church. What a contrast there is between the handling of the junction between pier and arch in, say, the presbytery of St Davids and what we see here! The secret lies in the complementary designs of the piers and the arches. At Llandaff and Llanthony it was achieved by the use of continuous orders. Cwmhir's piers have a square cross-section and they are orientated such that the V-shaped arch soffits continue naturally where the piers leave off. As well as carrying triple engaged shafts at the cardinal points, the piers carry four more clusters at the diagonals making twenty-four shafts in all. The centre one in each cluster carries a flat keel-mould, and the arches are richly roll-moulded to match the clustered piers beautifully to form almost continuous orders which are punctuated by elaborately-carved capitals. Moulded circular abaci and bases encourage the momentum as is the case with Brecon's presbytery, and this complete design displays

Fig. 147 Beddgelert. The nave arcade

the mastery of the Early English style. All of the elements come together to form an inevitable composition in a way which is rarely met with elsewhere, and one feels that here the style has realized its full potential.

Beddgelert

Beddgelert, like Penmon, appears to have remained a Celtic foundation which adopted the Augustinian Order early in the thirteenth century. The present church, largely rebuilt in the nineteenth century, contains a triplet of lancets in its east wall and a pair of arches leading into a north transept which are contemporary with the work at Cwmhir. The pier in the centre of

Figs. 148-149 Valle Crucis. The presbytery (top) and east front

the arches is octagonal, with single large engaged shafts on all eight faces, and the bell capitals and bases are boldly roll-moulded. The arches carry a rich combination of large and small rolls, two of which have keel-mouldings, and a keeled hood-mould forms an outer order. Obviously of the same era as Cwmhir's, these arches offer different solutions to the problems of design which one may well feel are less successful, the large engaged shafts composing less easily with the arch mouldings than do Cwmhir's busy clusters.

Valle Crucis

The Cistercian abbey of Valle Crucis has an Early English church which was begun soon after the house's founding in 1201. Here, the benefactor was Madoc ap Gruffydd Maelor, an ally of Llywelyn the Great. The transepts and presbytery date from the first quarter of the thirteenth century, and the nave and west front from the second quarter. The upper sections of the latter's walls and the gable rose window on the west front date from the early fourteenth century, rebuilding having become necessary after a bad fire in the mid-thirteenth.

Of fairly modest proportions, the church has north and south transepts, each with two square eastern chapels. The eastern arm is divided into two bays to form a presbytery and a sanctuary, and triple engaged vaulting shafts all carry the flatter type of keel-moulding. The sanctuary is lit by single large splayed lancets in the north and south walls, and the eastern wall carries three graduated lancets which have obtuse heads, only just pointed as is the case with St Davids' blind lancets in the same position. Above are two acutely pointed splayed lancets with hood-moulds which continue horizontally to form a string, and another string-course at their base divides the elevation into two. All these large openings must have allowed an impressive flood of light into the eastern end of the church, and the exterior face of the east wall shows how the need to reinforce it adequately, brought about by the number of large openings, was turned into architectural display. The buttresses are of the shallow pilaster type which have been nicely stylized to enclose the upper lancets, and a larger blind lancet has also been formed in the centre. The composition is therefore unusually elaborate, and the lower lancets also carry external decoration, the centre one shafted.

Fig. 150 Valle Crucis. The south transept chapels

The south transept chapels are well preserved, and the bold, square, stepped-ordered archways are complemented with unusual bases and piers which consist of clusters of polygons with convex faces, the forward faces projecting outwards slightly to form broad shallow rectangular mouldings which rise up to engage capitals of a similar design. Above the dressed stonework of the arches a band of undressed stone voussoirs form relieving arches which help to bear the load of the walls above. A complete contrast to the delicate work of Cwmhir and Beddgelert, this robust, successful design belongs more to the Margam and later Brecon schools, and the elaborate carving which was illustrated in chapter six (Figures 60-66) proclaims both the independent spirit of the Celts and the relaxation of the original Cistercian ideals.

The west front carries fenestration which is poised on the brink of becoming bar tracery. Three large graduated lancets were each subdivided by vertical mullions into two lights, and we can still see that those of the outer windows have trefoil cusped heads, above which are roundels which have been pierced with sexfoils. This is plate tracery that achieves a lightness of feel which is very similar to the bar tracery of Tintern Abbey's church, designed only a couple of decades later.

Continuous roll-mouldings enclose the windows, and a rather uneven halo which was disturbed during the later rebuilding forms a decorative hood-mould. The splay at the bases of the windows completes the frame, and buttresses flank the composition which counteracted the thrusts of the nave arcades. The rose window in the gable belongs to the fourteenth century, and above it is a Latin inscription which associates it with Abbot Adam who was Abbot of Valle Crucis between 1330 and 1344. The rose consists of eight panels of dagger motifs: trefoil-cusped lancets with sides which converge towards a point at the base, the dagger being a favourite motif in window tracery and timber and stone panel work of the Decorated period and after.

The interior face of the west front is very similar to the exterior, except that the doorway is plain. The windows are slightly more recessed with extra mouldings, and here the splay has now become a decorative device as much as a light-

Fig. 151 Valle Crucis. The west front

capturing one because the window sizes have increased compared with those of the earlier eastern end of the church, an early illustration in one building of how as time went on wall area decreased at the expense of ever-increasing window area.

Christ College Chapel, Brecon

Christ College, Brecon, was founded by Henry VIII in 1541, one of a number in Britain founded at the sites of dissolved convents in recognition of their role as educators. There are no records, however, of this particular friary having been engaged in educational work especially, and the dedication of the church to St Nicholas, the patron saint of children, was a coincidence which became appropriate only after the dissolution. The chapel was originally the choir of a Dominican friary, the founding of which is obscure, there being scant records of its life generally. It and the ruined choir of the Carmelite friary in Denbigh are the only substantial remains left by the friars in Wales. Brecon's was founded in about 1240, and its choir remains intact and in use. The walking place, the corridor in a friars' church that separated the nave from the choir and gave access to the conventual buildings, has been rebuilt and now forms an ante-chapel, and of the nave only some ruined walling and piers remain, the latter having formed an arcade to a north aisle. The east window consists of five graduated lancets which are formed by the use of bar tracery within an overall large pointed frame, and this is believed to have been inserted in the fourteenth century. The windows in the side walls consist of single lancets with the usual splays on the insides, and there is a triple sedilia and a double piscina, their cusped moulded heads being similar to those in the cathedral nearby.

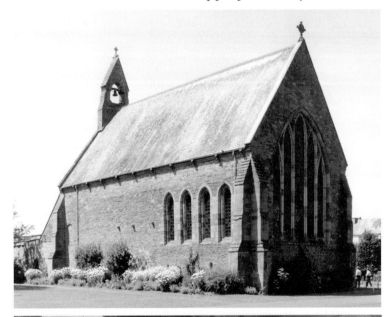

Figs. 152-153 Brecon. Christ College Chapel

This choir is plain, bright and functional, and although it is difficult to draw conclusions about the architecture of the friaries in general since so few examples have survived, one can at least tentatively suggest that the ideals of the friars are reflected in the remains at Brecon, Denbigh and Norwich: utilitarian designs which eschew architectural display. A remarkable survival from the days of the friary is the row of choir stalls, now placed in the ante-chapel, which dates probably from the early sixteenth century. Cruder misericords you will not see.

Figs. 154-158 Brecon. Christ College Chapel. Choir stalls carvings

10

Decorated

Tintern

The building work at the east end of Margam, begun in about 1200, illustrates the fact that the Cistercians had relaxed their austere ideals, and the church of Tintern Abbey shows just how unencumbered they had become by the late thirteenth century when it came to architectural display. The abbey was founded in 1131 by Walter FitzRichard de Clare, and very extensive remains can be seen today of both the church and the conventual buildings which were sited to the north. Wandering around these ruins it is here more than anywhere that one appreciates that an abbey was indeed a city in microcosm, and one is particularly impressed by the sheer number of buildings to the north-east which included a farmery (infirmary), kitchen, abbot's hall, an earlier abbot's house, his private lodgings complete with chapel, and a dovecot. Running through the complex is an extensive drainage system.

The church was completely rebuilt in the comparatively short space of about thirty years from about 1270, latterly under the patronage of Earl Roger Bigod III, who was also funding the building of some new accommodation at Chepstow Castle a few miles downriver. Efforts were usually made to disturb worship as little as possible during rebuilding programmes, and so Tintern's new church was built around the smaller Norman one as far as possible before the latter was finally dismantled. It fully demonstrates the way in which buildings of the Decorated period reflect a move towards a more extrovert, worldly outlook in society generally as well as among the monastic Orders, and so Tintern's church is a good building to look at first because it contrasts very markedly with the buildings covered so far.

Fig. 159 Tintern. The church, looking south-east

Mention has been made of the impact that Westminster Abbey, which was being rebuilt from 1245, had on the architecture of Britain generally, and at Tintern this is felt to a considerable extent. The church is lofty (although certainly not a rival of Westminster), geometric bar tracery fills large window openings, the high vault sprang from quite a low level to increase the sense of height as it reached up above the clerestories, and naturalistic foliage was introduced into the carving. Unlike at Westminster, no western towers were planned, and the east end remained emphatically square. Also, there is no gallery or tribune, a blank panel of walling occupying the space between the main arcade and the clerestory, which is punctuated only by vaulting shafts. This, and the relatively plain decorative detail, are characteristic of earlier Cistercian ideals. A feature so enjoyable about the elevations is the way in which the vaulting springs right from the bases of the very tall clerestories, and the ribs had to climb a considerable distance as they reached across to meet at the apex of the vault. An effect would have been created which drew the eye ever upwards towards the vault's climax at the roof bosses, and one only regrets that the triple engaged vaulting shafts only sprang from the ground in the transepts so that the opportunity for a continuous sweep from ground level to apex in the nave and eastern arm was missed, and instead, the shafts are supported by foliated corbels just above the piers of the arcades. The piers are quite slender for such tall elevations, and their eight shafts are grouped so that again the arches can continue the lines, a technique which was demonstrated so confidently at Cwmhir. Here again, round bell capitals assist the transition, and they support arches which have a larger cross-sectional area at the points of springing than do the piers, emphasizing the latter's slenderness. Arch mouldings are very rich in the transept and presbytery where the altars were, simpler ones being provided in the nave.

The clerestories are of two lights with trefoil cusped heads, and a sexfoiled roundel is placed above. Shallow splays, decorative now as much as functional, are enclosed by acutely pointed segmental arches with shafts to each side, the whole being framed by the vaulting ribs. The enormous east window, one of the largest in its time, was originally of eight lights with a complex pattern of geometric tracery in the head, and similar huge areas of fenestration flooded the crossing with light from the transepts' end walls, the lower section of the one to the north being blocked by the monks' dorter. Clearly, the master mason was supremely confident about the window areas which his walls could allow, and the experiment at the west front of Valle Crucis bore much fruit at Tintern.

The great west window of about 1300 stylistically occupies that brief point between pure geometric tracery, based upon circles and implied circles which are placed against or in between supporting tracery bars which continue the lines of the lancets into the head of the window, and fully curvilinear or flamboyant tracery, where the mullions themselves rise up to depart from their natural lines to form complex sinuous patterns. The tracery motifs are instead formed from short arcs of circles which are arranged to create acutely pointed forms of trefoil, quatrefoil and the like, and such tracery can be seen in contemporary work in the chapter houses of Wells, York and Southwell, in the great east window of Ripon, and as blind arcading in the towers of Salisbury, Hereford and Lichfield Cathedrals. The supreme example, however, even in ruin, is at Tintern. Of seven lights with trefoil cusped heads, the west window is divided into groups of two, three and two openings, and thicker mullions rise up to form three large graduated lancets, the centre one interrupted by

the roundel in the head of the window. Further interlocking lancet patterns are created by the continuation of the two central mullions, and immediately above the main lights a row of seven pointed trefoils have been formed by arcs of circles to create a flame-like effect. Two roundels above are each filled with a ring of conventional trefoils, and all of the remaining space is developed with a variety of little patterns. Here we see the master mason indulging in design for its own sake, structural necessity dictating what is artistically possible to a lesser extent than had previously been the case.

Beneath the window is the west door which consists of two trefoil-headed openings, the spandrel filled with blind arcading beneath a moulded arch which is echoed in miniature to either side. A vesica-shape in the centre above the doorway forms a saint-niche which would probably have contained a statue of the Virgin Mary, to whom all Cistercian churches were dedicated. The remains of the narthex can be seen just forward of the west front.

With such high clerestory walls with a vault, one might have expected to see flying buttresses, but in fact only two were constructed to support the east wall of the north transept. The reason for their absence is that the vaulting

Figs. 160-161 Tintern. The west front and detail of the west door

sprang from such a low level that its outward thrusts would have developed only a little above the line of the bases of the clerestories, allowing the large areas of thick walling to provide substantial mass-loading above the vault springers. This stabilizing weight from above, aided a little by external pilaster buttresses, obviated the need for any external support. Tintern's church represents another milestone in the understanding of forces in equilibrium, and the delicacy of style which could develop from it is worlds away from the naves of Chepstow, Ewenny and St Woolos. Today, we can build a frame of RSJs (rolled steel joists) and hang more or less what we want from it, being able to separate aesthetic considerations from structural integrity completely, but in medieval times the two developed very much hand in hand.

The usual design changes were made at Tintern as the building progressed, even though the church was completed in only thirty years or so. A new master mason is considered to have designed the west window, the cloister processional doorway, and the later aisle windows. The easternmost window in the south nave aisle is the same size as those in the presbytery, but the three to the west of it are taller whilst retaining identical tracery. The two westernmost bays contain smaller and higher windows which were the last to be built on this side, being of two lights with trefoil cusping. The roundel above is now a

Fig. 162 Tintern. The church, looking west

quatrefoil, unusually orientated so that its lobes point diagonally, and inside there are very tall shallow splays beneath the openings. The height of these windows suggests a special use for the western end of the south aisle, which also has its own west door. It is probable therefore that this part of the nave was used as an outer parlour to do business with the lay-community, the smaller windows giving a degree of privacy. The north aisle windows are of the same type, their smallness accommodating the cloisters to the north.

The old church would have been demolished at about this stage so that the north transept could be completed, and here one sees fragments of more complex forms of tracery in the windows. The processional doorway, which leads from the cloister to the nave, dates from a little after 1300, and it is elaborately cusped and moulded (Fig. 164). It is enclosed by a continuous order of diapers which take the form of stylized flowers, and a band of continuous roll-mouldings completes the decoration. Above is a trefoil with pointed lobes of a type similar to those in the west window.

The development of foliage design can be seen in the roof boss examples illustrated (Figs. 165-166). They decorated the junctions between the ribs in the high vault. The stiff-leaf foliage of the first is already familiar and is characteristic of Early English work, but the

Fig. 163 Tintern. The presbytery, looking south

Fig. 164 Tintern. The doorway leading from the cloisters into the nave

Figs. 165-166 Tintern. Roof bosses

Neath
Figs. 167-169 A capital from the church
(above), roof boss (top right), the corbel above
the night stairs (right)

second shows an example of the more naturalistic forms which were developed during the latter decades of the thirteenth century. Comparisons with work at Neath show how development progressed. The monks here were rebuilding their church between 1280 and 1330 as has been said, and its plan is very similar to Tintern's. The transepts had two eastern chapels, the presbytery was of four bays with aisles which formed an ambulatory behind the high altar, uncommon in Wales, and walling existed between the piers. The nave was of seven bays compared with Tintern's six, and again there was an elaborate west door with flanking blind arcading. The nave pier and clerestory designs resembled Tintern's, and both nave aisles had doorways to the west. Very like Tintern then, the two churches must have made a magnificent pair. Neath's vaulting boss illustrates further stylistic developments: Christ in Glory is set within a quatrefoil, the latter decorated with ballflowers, a stylized flower which consists of a bulbous head with an incised trefoil suggesting the opening of petals to reveal a smaller bulbous form within. The ballflower became the dominant decorative motif of the later Decorated period (except in northern parts of England where it is rather more scarce), just as the dogtooth had dominated Early English work. Naturalistic foliage sprouts from the quatrefoil and here the leaves have become undulating, very different from the pre-1300 example at Tintern. Another example of the undulating naturalistic leaf decorates a capital from the church, its stem forming a spiral-moulded annulet around

the shaft (Fig. 167), and one can see that the formality of Early English work has been completely forsaken for an exuberance which is the hallmark of the late Decorated style. Above the night stair is a delightful carved corbel (Fig. 169).

Brecon

The nave rebuilding of Brecon Cathedral was begun in the last years of the thirteenth century, and how different it is from Tintern and Neath. Here is Decorated work in a more minor key, but there can be no denying its beauty. Compared with Tintern, Brecon's later Decorated work shows how overall design consistency was relaxed over an extended building period, the window tracery developed into more ambitious and varied forms, and decoration became more flamboyant. Earlier Decorated work continued under a discipline which the Early English phase had used to great effect, but at Brecon we see how each feature of the nave appears to be a compartment in itself, divorced from an overall concept. The aisle windows, the

Fig. 170 Brecon Cathedral.
The nave, looking west

Figs. 171-172 Brecon Cathedral. St Keyne's Chapel (left) and tomb canopy in the chapel (right)

north clerestories, the south clerestories, the west window, and the tomb canopy are all individual designs in themselves, although Exeter demonstrated how successfully stylistic unity could be wrought from these apparently wayward forms.

The south arcade of Brecon's nave is simpler than the north, and it is the earlier of the two. The nave is short, only four bays on the north side and three on the south, with an additional blank bay of Norman walling just west of the crossing. The clerestories have been placed above the main arcades' piers rather than the arches in order to develop a horizontal pull to this short nave, and there is no blind-storey. The aisle windows are unusual for the date in having mullions which reach right up until they meet the head of the arch, this being a strong characteristic of Perpendicular fenestration, and the west window of the south aisle shows an example of reticulated double ogee tracery: the repetition of a pattern to create a net-like effect. The great west window develops the theme, its five lights carrying cinquefoil cusping, the roundel above containing four quatrefoils which have been elongated, this technique fully exploited in the tracery lights to either side. The south clerestory windows have simple interlocking tracery of a late thirteenth-century type, the curves of the three lancets simply continuing into the head of the window to form a series of Y patterns; the later north clerestories are more complex, displaying alternating examples of the later tracery of the period.

The eastern bay of the north aisle of the nave now forms St Keyne's Chapel, and the timber screen which separates it from the nave originally enclosed the choir (Fig. 171). It is decorated with bosses from the fifteenth-century roof which is still in position above the presbytery vaulting.

A tomb recess with an effigy in St Keyne's Chapel (Fig. 172) probably belongs to the patron of the rebuilding of the nave, and it is typical of late Decorated design. The canopy forms a broad ogee, and there are two bands of ballflower decoration among the rich stepped mouldings. There is multiple cusping, the central compartment itself forming an ogee curve to complement the hood. The rare dormer window above again shows an example of reticulated tracery, the two main compartments formed out of circles which have been drawn out to ogees at the bottom. Similar work can be seen in the doorway of the Havard Chapel.

Fenestration: Llandaff, Bangor, St Davids

The aisle windows of the nave at Llandaff are very unusual in that the windows themselves are ogees. The reticulated double ogee tracery has been given quatrefoil cusping to enrich the effect, and segments of tracery around the periphery suggest a continuation of the reticulation beyond the window itself. The nave aisle windows of Bangor Cathedral which are a little earlier are rather more conservative, with the lower quatrefoils set within

Fig. 173 Llandaff.
Nave aisle window

Fig. 174 Bangor. The south face

133

Fig. 175 St Davids Cathedral. The south face of the nave

Fig. 176 Llandaff.
The east window

circles, and the whole design is firmly enclosed inside the confines of the opening (Fig. 174). St Davids' nave aisle windows are nineteenth-century restorations of the original tracery, and here we see alternating designs (Fig. 175). The first and third windows make use of double interlocking ogees which form roundels above, the other two echoing Brecon's south clerestories but with an enrichment of elaborate cusping. One of the most complex and fascinating late Decorated windows is to be found above the high altar at Llandaff (Fig. 176). Of three lights, transoms divide the window in half with the lower sections filled with blind arcading, this anticipating Perpendicular panelling. Cinquefoil cusped ogee heads are further enriched with cusping in the spandrels, and above there are three similar ogees which develop into an elaborate roundel filled with three spherical triangles. Set within each of these is a trefoil upon which a three-pointed star has been superimposed, the points of which reach into the corners of the triangles. This latter motif is a strong characteristic of designs much found in south-eastern England. The remaining tracery lights are all cusped, and the whole composition is set within a moulded arch. Naturalistic foliage decorates the capitals of the arch piers, but unfortunately it is much too small to be appreciated from the ground. The window is flanked by smaller blind arcades, and an attractive balustrade with quatrefoil piercings runs around the base of all of the clerestories in the presbytery. Above the east window there is a splayed hood-moulded roundel, and this is decorated with a ring of ballflowers.

St Asaph

At St Asaph, the north transept's end window consists of no less than four interlocking ogees which develop into cusped elliptical reticulation, and in the tower we see a rare instance of a mason of a later age complementing it in the bell openings. The top section of the tower had to be rebuilt following storm damage in 1714 (the later brickwork can be clearly seen) but the renewed tracery is believed to have been to the original design. The transoms which divide the main openings, and the cinquefoil cusping in the roundel, are the only obvious Perpendicular features. The great west window is another good example of the remarkable effect which can be produced by the repetition of simple graceful patterns, the elaborate cusping busying the eye amongst what is in fact a straightforward florid design. The doorway beneath consists of continuous orders of sunken chamfers, that is chamfers which are let into the stone a little to create ridges at the boundaries of the moulding. It is a rather uninspired design, but the sunken chamfer is used with telling effect in the window tracery above.

Fig. 177 St Asaph. The tower and north transept

The Decorated nave and transepts of St Asaph were built following the damage done to the Norman cathedral by the Earl of Warwick during bishop Anian II's episcopate, the war between Edward I and Llywelyn the Last bringing with it damage to many religious houses. The rebuilding work progressed slowly throughout much of the fourteenth century, the tower was built in 1391 by the master mason Robert Fagan, and the multi-foiled square clerestories were added in 1403. Further destruction had been wrought at the hands of Owain Glyndŵr in 1402, the eastern arm this time being the principal victim, and the presbytery seen today was largely reconstructed in the original Early English style by Scott in the nineteenth century. It contains a good set of choir stalls of the late fifteenth century.

St Asaph's nave arcade piers are robust affairs for Decorated work, and they are memorable for their continuous orders of wave mouldings: broad very shallow rolls flanked by two much smaller hollow rolls, so that in cross-section the moulding forms a gentle wave. The master

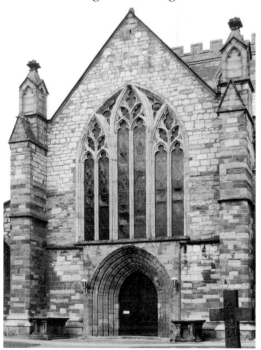

Fig. 178 St Asaph. The west front

135

Fig. 179 St Asaph. The nave

Fig. 180 St Asaph. The late fifteenth-century choir stalls

mason Walter of Hereford had employed it earlier in Caernarfon Castle, and his successor Henry of Ellerton built the castle's King's Gate from about 1315 which again makes use of the wave around its archway. It will be seen again at Valle Crucis, and it is another example of regional influence which was also encountered a century or so earlier in the south with the pollarded willow capital. But the wave moulding found favour throughout Britain (Chester Abbey and Wells Cathedral employed it soon after Caernarfon, and the pulpitum and south aisle windows of St Davids also have it), and in it we see a flattening of the surface compared with the mouldings at, say, Cwmhir, Tintern and Brecon, and this indeed became the trend. In the wave mouldings at St Asaph, boldly projecting articulation has given way to surface ripples; they do not cast deep shadows, and the texture has become smooth.

Valle Crucis

The magnificent chapter house at Valle Crucis is stylistically quite similar to St Asaph's nave. It is built on a square plan, and vaulted in nine compartments to form a central aisle with two equal side aisles. Belonging to the mid-fourteenth century, the chapter house makes use of continuous orders in the vaulting, the wave-moulded ribs

Fig. 181 Valle Crucis. The chapter house

Fig. 182 Valle Crucis. The chapter house book cupboard

Fig. 183 Kidwelly. Window and sedilia in the presbytery

flowing into the piers which then spread to form the bases in a manner very similar to St Asaph's nave piers, the completely unbroken lines also dying into the walls without the use of corbels. It is an assured design, the master mason allowing no punctuation anywhere which would only have disturbed the rhythm of his conception. The reticulated east windows are very much of their age, the central one being a nineteenth-century re-creation which can be believed. To the north of the entrance doorway, which has two continuous wave-moulded orders, there is a book cupboard. It consists of a central doorway with flanking alcoves which were provided for the books, and all three openings have very depressed cusped ogee heads, the depressed arch being a much favoured form in arcading and window tracery of the Perpendicular period. Immediately above each of these is a pair of cusped openings. The dagger motif was encountered in the rose high up in the church's west front, and here the dagger has been given a curling blade to form what is known as a mouchette, and it was used a great deal in window and timber panel tracery from the fourteenth century onwards. The upper section of the opening is formed by two conventional interlocking ogees, these complemented by inverted interlocking ogees to form the roundel above.

Kidwelly
At Kidwelly, the window above the sedilia also makes use of the mouchette (see Valle Crucis, above), and here the cusped tracery lights radiate from a central point. Kidwelly Priory was founded early in the twelfth century as a Benedictine cell of Sherborne Abbey in Dorset; the mother house impresses chiefly for its Perpendicular fan vaulting and some of the arches which survive from the earlier Saxon cathedral, but Kidwelly impresses with its late Decorated east end. The presbytery has no aisles, and it is about ten feet narrower than the broad aisle-less nave. The Valle Crucis chapter house demonstrated how rich could be the effect just with the use of simple forms, and the

Kidwelly sedilia also achieves its effect with a remarkable economy of means. The triangular-headed bays are made up of simple chamfered square members, these continuing through the seating to meet the semi-octagonal bases; there is cusping in the triangular spandrels, and that is about it. Yet how rich the effect is, the lovely white limestone contributing greatly to the bright, ethereal atmosphere of this church's eastern arm.

A plain chantry chapel is built onto the north wall of the presbytery, and it gives access to a stairway, built into the thickness of the wall, which leads to an anchorite cell; an anchorite was a person who lived a hermit-like existence of religious meditation. Pierced in the wall of this cell is a small window opening through

Fig. 184 Kidwelly. Anchorite cell window, high up in the presbytery

which he, or indeed she, could view the high altar, and it has been given a swirl of tracery.

All of these examples of the Decorated style show how artistic design had come to be indulged in for its own sake, and the trend was of course universal throughout Britain. The important Decorated work at St Davids Cathedral again illustrates the extrovert nature of this age, and also how a powerful bishop could leave his mark upon the fabric of his cathedral.

Fig. 185 St Davids Cathedral. The pulpitum

St Davids

Henry de Gower was bishop of St Davids between 1328 and 1347, and he instigated some of the most beautiful Decorated work in Britain. During his episcopate important buildings were erected at the bishop's palaces of St Davids and Lamphey, and at the cathedral there are the tombs in the Lady Chapel and the nave, the south door, the remodelling of St Thomas's Chapel with the addition of a chapter house over (now the library), the eastward extension of the presbytery aisles, the heightening of the nave and presbytery aisle walls, their fenestration, the pulpitum, and the middle stage of the tower. He left quite a legacy.

Many pulpitums have perished, and we are fortunate that first-class Decorated examples have survived at Exeter, Lincoln and Southwell. The one at St Davids belongs with this select group, and it is the epitome of its age. Placed about mid way along the easternmost bay of the nave, the pulpitum contains Gower's tomb set amidst lavish carving, and either side of the central doorway are niches containing modern effigies, the one to the south being St David, above which are nodding ogees: the ogee-shaped hoods bow forwards a little to form a canopy over the statues. The central doorway leads to a passage which has skeletal vaulting above, the ribs forming open flying tracery without an infill of webbing. Gower's tomb contains beautiful examples of undulating naturalistic leaf carving, the arches are elaborately cusped to form delicate patterns of open 'drop' tracery, and flamboyant crockets decorate them. The north end of the pulpitum is supported by a shallow flying buttress with cusped open tracery, and the north-west face has a doorway with an unusual semi-octagonal head, this formed by four chamfered cants which join to form a continuous order around the door (Fig. 188). Cinquefoil cusping accompanies the original fourteenth-century ironwork, and to the left is a plain ogee-headed piscina.

The south nave door is elaborately carved with sculptured decoration which represents the Tree of Jesse, but the porch, an afterthought, came too

Figs. 186-187 St Davids Cathedral. Bishop Gower's tomb

late to save it from the severe weathering which has obliterated most of the detail. It is still just possible to discern the figure of Adam with Eve issuing from his side on the western impost, and on the eastern side is a recumbent figure of Jesse from whom springs a branch to form a series of compartments around the doorway within which are set figures of his descendents.

St Thomas Becket's Chapel lies to the east of the north transept, and it has a thirteenth-century double piscina. Otherwise it is a Decorated remodelling, and the complex vaulting is an example of the *tierceron* type (Fig. 189). Apart from the usual ribs of a quadripartite vault there are additional tiercerons which meet the ridge rib at oblique angles, and further ribs spring to meet not with the ridge but with secondary ribs, the latter reaching from the window openings to the apex. The vault is in two bays and is supported by semi-octagonal engaged shafts with foliated capitals, and the windows have quite deep splays which are enclosed by triangular-headed arches. This attractive vault sports some good bosses which feature both heads and

Fig. 188 St Davids Cathedral. The north face of the pulpitum with flying buttress on the right

foliage, and it indeed forms a glade of stone, as that ever-colourful writer and architect Hugh Braun would say. He is right to draw our attention to a vault's representation of tree branches forming a canopy above our heads, and the early sixteenth century vaulting in the organ gallery of Prague Cathedral (probably by Benedict Reith) proclaims the source of its inspiration with naturalistically imitated branches forming the ribs. Another complex and attractive vault can be seen in St Davids' Lady Chapel, a *lierne* vault belonging to the twentieth-century restoration (Fig. 190). This particular example is similar to a fan vault but with the addition of liernes, short extra ribs which link the structural ones to form decorative patterns without themselves contributing structurally.

Above the Becket Chapel are two further floors which form a tower-like structure, this reaching above the level of the transept. It projects at a slight angle. The upper two storeys now comprise a library and a gallery, and the complex fenestration incorporates

Fig. 189 St Davids Cathedral. The St Thomas Becket Chapel vault

Fig. 190 *St Davids Cathedral. The Lady Chapel vault*

Fig. 191 *St Davids Cathedral. The St Thomas Becket Chapel with the library and gallery above*

double ogee tracery. The gallery is lit by a window which takes the form of a spherical triangle, within which are set three similar smaller cusped triangles.

The central stage of the crossing tower forms a lantern within, the elaborately cusped window openings lighting the timber ceiling which dates from about 1500. Originally this ceiling was lower, cutting off the upper sections of the windows, but Scott in his nineteenth-century restoration raised it so that all of the window area could give light. He asked our forgiveness for tampering with the original design here, but surely he was right. At the base of this lantern stage in each corner are springers in preparation for a stone vault, but fortunately the scheme was abandoned in favour of this impressively lit timber roof above the choir.

Parallels have been drawn between Gower's work and contemporary designs in western England, particularly Bristol's St Mary Redcliffe church and the Augustinian abbey which became the cathedral

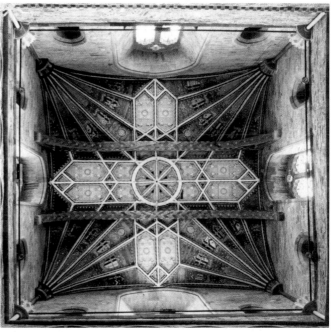

Fig. 192 *St Davids Cathedral. The lantern tower*

141

after the dissolution. A badly weathered tomb in St Davids' south nave aisle has a striking star-patterned canopy of the type which is also found at Redcliffe, and the north porch of the latter has a similarly impressive star-canopied doorway, the porch itself being built upon a hexagonal plan with radiating buttresses at the corners. Mention can also be made of the skeletal vault in the entrance vestibule to Bristol Cathedral's Berkeley Chapel which resembles the Gower pulpitum's, and the octagonal-headed doorway in the latter finds a companion in Berkeley Castle a few miles from Bristol. Abbot Edmund Knowle ruled Bristol Abbey during the first third of the fourteenth century, and it was he who was responsible for commissioning the daringly original work which one sees there. Unfortunately the name of the master mason is not known, but the facts that Gower was a friend of Knowle's, and that the work at St Davids immediately followed that at Bristol, gives the link. The St Davids designs are generally more conventional and 'mainstream' than the fantastic creations at Bristol, and it is probable that a senior mason working on the latter became a master mason in his own right to design the St Davids work, bringing Bristol influences with him.

The octagonal profiles and star patterns (particularly in the porch of St Mary Redcliffe) betray Saracenic influences, and these had earlier played a part in the improvements in masonry-craft evident in Britain after about 1100. The influence again here must have been catalysed by the Crusade of Edward I between 1270 and 1274, and in 1289 envoys of the Mongol Ilkhan of Persia visited London. This was followed up two years later by Sir Geoffrey Langley's travels to the Middle East, Langley having accompanied Edward on the Crusades, and these and other trading contacts amply account for the flow of influences. Bristol was a busy sea port even then.

Bishop's Palaces: St Davids and Lamphey
Bishop Gower instigated important building programmes at the bishop's palaces of St Davids and Lamphey, and work at Swansea Castle was also carried out by him. The chief characteristic common to all of these works is the use of the arcaded parapet: at St Davids the arcades of pointed arches are decorated with chequer work, Swansea's are

Fig. 193 St Davids, bishop's palace

142

Fig. 194 Lamphey. The gatehouse

Fig. 195 St Davids, bishop's palace.
Detail of the parapet

formed out of startlingly bright limestone, and at Lamphey the arches are rounded to form what is in effect another appearance of a Romanesque arcade. Surely St Davids' Cathedral tower would also have displayed this feature before the upper stage was added in a later era. Again, it must be remembered that the rubble walling which surrounds the arcades was once plastered, and in their day they must have made a considerably more impressive sight than they do now. Above them were embattled sections of walling with arrow loop piercings, these contributing aesthetically rather than defensively. Yet so striking a design found no favour elsewhere, and it remained a localized phenomenon.

The chapel at St Davids even has its own tower and spire, the latter being of the broach type: it is octagonal, and small pyramidal buttresses against the diagonals, known as broaches, assist the union between tower and spire. A corbel table runs around the spire's base, and the tower once contained two bells. The other common form of spire is the parapet type, this meeting the tower entirely within the confines of a parapet such that no part of its base can be seen, and Llandaff has an example.

Apart from the south range of buildings which were built by Gower, there are the remains of

Fig. 196 Lamphey. The undercroft of Bishop Gower's great hall

Fig. 197 St Davids, bishop's palace. The chapel

an earlier west range and an eastern range which contains both Gower's and later work, but his arcaded parapets everywhere are the chief memorable feature. At Lamphey the parapet decorates another great hall and the gatehouse, and again Gower's contribution is the main attraction amongst both earlier and later work.

Denbigh

The last chapter ended with a look at the Dominican friary at Brecon, and the friary at Denbigh, the only Carmelite house to be founded in Wales, can end the present one. Sir John Salusbury of Lleweni, who died in 1289, is believed to have been the founder of the friary, and the buildings which remain were built in about 1300. It is situated about a mile away from the centre of the medieval town, this probably due to the fact that the Carmelites were closer to the monastic Orders than were the other Orders of friars, and a certain amount of privacy was presumably desired. The remains consist of a choir whose walls stand to a good height, and to the west are sections of walling which comprised the walking place and the nave. Substantial remains of the north and east windows have been bricked up in recent times to preserve their tracery, and a good impression of the choir can thereby still be gleaned. The north window is unusual, comprising a row of five equal openings with ogee heads set within a frame without any splays. The top of the frame forms a very gently curved segmental arch. The deep mullions which divide the five lights are each pierced with two narrow transverse openings (that is parallel to the wall), one above the other, and these have trefoil cusping and ogee heads. Blind versions decorate the end reveals, and the window glazing was fitted just to the rear of these piercings. Brecon Friary's church received a large east window in the fourteenth century, and at Denbigh a Perpendicular window, which almost entirely fills the east wall, was fitted in the same position in about 1400. It is a typical product of the Perpendicular period with its straightforward open rectangular panelling, and it would have flooded this small choir with light.

Fig. 198 Denbigh. The choir of the Carmelite friary

11

Perpendicular

The Decorated style, lavish, inventive, and extrovert, developed and flourished not coincidentally during the reigns of Henry III and Edward I. The former was an enthusiastic patron of the church and therefore of its artistic endeavours, ever open to European and particularly French ideas; and the latter became one of the most dominant and highly respected monarchs of Europe. But Edward spent fortunes not on the church but on military campaigns, and this encouraged the church to turn its own assets into a form which could not easily be requisitioned by him: new building work. Edward II's reign was something of an anticlimax to say the least (although his tomb in Gloucester Cathedral demonstrates no corresponding flagging of Decorated invention) but by the 1330s the young King Edward III had begun to revitalize the English monarchy. Like his grandfather, he proved himself an able military leader but he showed little interest in winning minds as well as victories in France. Culturally therefore the Hundred Years War isolated Britain from Europe (Scotland maintained links with France, England being the common enemy) and she developed a rather more insular artistic outlook as a result — the resultant Perpendicular style was peculiar to Britain. The Black Death of the years around 1349 took a heavy toll, and craftsmen suffered as much as anyone else, but the move away from complex window tracery, flamboyant decorative stone carving and sumptuous surface treatments can be detected well before this. At Gloucester, the presbytery shows just how rapidly the new style had developed, contemporary as it was with Bishop Gower's work at St Davids, Exeter Cathedral, and work at Brecon, Neath, Wells, Bristol, and Selby Abbey. The work at Gloucester predates the Black Death, and even that stemmed from earlier innovations at St Stephen's Chapel in the Palace of Westminster and the chapter house and cloisters of Old St Paul's Cathedral. The loss of the latter two buildings in fires encouraged a tendency to believe that Perpendicular was a kind of expedient as a result of the Black Death, relinquishing as it does the delicate, complex artistry and craftsmanship displayed in, say, Gower's tomb. But Gloucester's audacious presbytery demolishes the theory.

The fifteenth-century north aisle window of Newport Cathedral sums up the new style (Fig. 199). It is almost identical to contemporary windows at Usk. The double ogee compartments have been stretched out to give straight sides, and the ogees themselves have been converted into triangular forms. The window is regularly panelled, and larger examples such as the one at Denbigh feature transoms which divide the main lights up

Fig. 199 Newport. North nave aisle window

into more panelling. Tastes change, and it is impossible to look back six hundred years in an attempt to understand why, say, the aisle windows of Llandaff were relinquished for the aisle windows of Newport. But the former are not intrinsically more beautiful than the latter, and when one considers the loss of virtually all medieval glass in Wales, Newport's window begins to be understood. It is designed specifically for the display of stained glass. The tracery itself does not merit attention, but today attention is thrown unfairly upon it.

The late Decorated style had become earthbound. Compared with the presbytery of Brecon and the church of Tintern Abbey, which contain strong devotional characteristics with their pure, reaching lines supported by complementary continuous mouldings, the busy decorative work of St Davids, Llandaff and Kidwelly embodies artistry of a different kind. It is divorced from the structure. Verticality has gone, the lines have been deliberately broken up with ballflowers, foliage, and wayward tracery which eschews the use of circles, and the dignity which comes with overall cohesion of design has been lost. The Perpendicular style can be seen as a reaction against this, and a fresh outlook of consistency and even repetition restored the principle of the complete concept which focused attention upon the whole rather than upon the part. And the vertical line was ruthlessly reinstated. But this is not to say that interest in aesthetics waned. On the contrary. The latter half of the fourteenth century saw the rebuilding of the great naves of Canterbury and Winchester Cathedrals for example, and the Perpendicular period produced many of the most ambitious tomb canopies, chantry chapels, towers, and vaults. But the artistry was more formal, and it was certainly more disciplined.

There are very few wholly Perpendicular cathedrals or monastic churches in Britain, Bath Abbey being the most overt example, and it reflects the fact that by this last phase of the Gothic period the process of updating, enlarging and re-fitting rather than building or re-building anew had become firmly established. Bangor Cathedral is the only substantially Perpendicular church in Wales among the buildings dealt with here, and if one seeks complete buildings in the style, one can do no better than to turn to the impressive group of parish churches of the fifteenth and early sixteenth centuries, and the building of these was funded not only by the established church and its traditional patrons, but also by the rich landowners who had substantial local interests and influence. Their money was now going to their parish church, and the cathedral and abbey was patronized less by them. Excellent Perpendicular churches include St Marcella at Llanfarchell near Denbigh, St Giles at Wrexham, All Saints at Gresford, and St Mary's at Mold. St John's in Cardiff is another fine example, and all of these churches can be said to outshine Bangor Cathedral in both the quality of their architecture and the richness of the decoration.

This last chapter therefore consists mainly of sections dealing with towers, porches, tombs and choir stalls, and the formality of the Perpendicular style which is common to all of the above makes an interesting contrast with the Decorated work of the previous chapter. But first, we will look at Bangor itself.

Bangor

Bangor Cathedral was another victim of Owain Glyndŵr's revolt, and the building today contains just a section of the old Norman church in the south presbytery wall. Much of the presbytery, the transepts and the central tower belong to Scott's nineteenth-century restoration, and the meagre upper section of the latter was built in the 1960s after a rather more ambitious scheme had to be abandoned because of doubts about the foundations. The nave aisle walls belong to the early fourteenth century, and the nave arcades, clerestories and west tower date from the early sixteenth.

The nave arcades make use of the four-centred arch which appeared in Britain in the early fourteenth century, but became popular in the late fifteenth. Its very depressed profile is the antithesis of the lancet, but the almost rectangular opening which it creates made it useful also for doorways. It is not a very transcendental profile in itself, but many late medieval churches which make use of the four-centred arch in arcading exploit its almost

Fig. 200 Bangor. The nave

rectangular profile by utilizing great height which allows huge aisle windows to flood the church with light. But Bangor's nave arcades are modest, the aisle windows are not large, and the advantages of this arch profile have not been exploited here. The clerestories are very squat, and they too have a four-centred profile, the simple tracery recalling Brecon's aisle windows. On the exterior they are enclosed within a large shallow hollow roll, and the west tower bell openings are taller versions of the clerestories. Large shallow rolls also form continuous orders around the archway which leads from the nave to the tower, and all of these similar mouldings assist the unity of the design.

The great east window dates from about 1500 and it is typically Perpendicular. The mullions reach right up to the head of the

Fig. 201 Lamphey. The chapel's east window

Fig. 202 Bangor. This oak carving of about 1500 is an example of a Bound Rood, depicting Jesus immediately before the crucifixion

Figs. 203-204 Fifteenth-century fonts: Chepstow (left) and Bangor

Fig. 206 Newport. The tower of St Woolos contains thirteen bells, the largest peal in Wales

Fig. 207 Bangor. The west tower, from an engraving of 1818 by H.S. Storer

window, and the rectangular open panels facilitate the display of the glass. Later windows tended to be broader with less acutely pointed heads, and the east window in the chapel at the Lamphey bishop's palace is more typical of the sixteenth century: hardly pointed at all, the tracery now achieves a serenity for which the final, Tudor phase of the Perpendicular style is known.

Towers

The last phase of Gothic architecture can boast some splendid towers, and the famous Somerset group find stylistic parallels in south Wales. The Jasper tower at Llandaff is one of the best examples of the style with its (restored) complex parapet of pierced crenellations and the cluster of pinnacles. This three-stage tower has a boldly projecting polygonal stair turret, and massive stepped angle buttresses create a powerful thrust of upward movement towards the crown. Newport's fifteenth-century tower is also of three stages with a projecting turret, and here we see examples of single diagonal buttresses. Bangor's west tower is rather more squat. Built in 1532, it again features diagonal buttresses. Monkton's fifteenth-century tower (Fig. 208) is a good example of the Pembrokeshire style, its tall, slender profile uncompromised by buttressing or the presence of large window or bell openings. The stair turret is carried up above the tower's projecting parapet, the latter supported by a corbel table. It is a most attractive tower. The origins of the style date from the early twelfth century when Flemings, mainly coming from original settlements in East Anglia, colonized parts of Pembrokeshire following the Norman invasions. They built their church towers with

Fig. 205 Llandaff. The Jasper tower parapet

Fig. 208 Monkton. The tower

Fig. 209 St Davids Cathedral. The tower

defence in mind, developing tall, windowless, inaccessible structures within which the villagers could take refuge during Welsh raids, and Celtic round towers which survive in Ireland and Scotland were built for similar defensive purposes. Simple stone vaults were also sometimes built to protect a church against fire. Pembroke's is an example of a form born of utilitarian necessity which developed into a regional style, betraying little of its original root.

The three-stage tower at St Davids reflects building programmes in the early thirteenth, fourteenth and sixteenth centuries. The plain lower stage is separated from the next by a string-course of ballflowers, and nook-shafts rise up to meet double octagonal shafts in the corners of the upper stage. Single polygonal shafts decorate the faces of this stage to complement, and they all carry annulets. The large Decorated openings of the central stage are flanked by niches with cinquefoiled ogee canopies, these embellished with crockets and poppyheads. The austere top stage is a disappointment, but the attractive pierced parapet carries a set of eight hexagonal pinnacles, the ridges of each decorated with shafts and moulded capitals. The latter support rings of winged grotesques, and the pinnacles are capped with ogee cupolas.

Abergavenny's tower is a rather stark, robust affair.

The porches at Usk

In the fifteenth century the nun's church at Usk received north and west porches, the fenestration was updated, and timber screens were built. The porches are fascinating. The north one was built in about 1460, and the badge in the centre of the parapet, which contains a drawbridge, suggests that the patron could have been Lord Herbert of Raglan. The west porch has no such crest, and there are as many differences as there are similarities between the two. They are both built with finely jointed dressed stone, which contrasts with the rubble work of the church. Both have triangular buttresses supporting the side walls, but

*Figs. 210-212 The porches at Usk. The west porch (top left), north porch (top right)
and detail of the parapet of the north porch*

the north porch has horizontal string-courses in addition. Its parapet carries a pattern of crosses within squares within cusped compartments, but the west parapet has a series of quatrefoils set within both circles and squares. They are similarly vaulted, but the north porch's vault is rather more steeply pitched. The latter has lateral buttresses to the front, but the west porch has diagonal buttresses. The moulded doorways are similarly decorated, but the poppyhead finial and crockets of the west porch are flatter and more formal. Its arch springs from a higher point than does the north one, and it is more depressed. The flatter vault of the west porch, the design of its parapet and the less acutely pointed archway all look forward to the sixteenth century, and it is perhaps the later of the two.

The Tombs, Abergavenny

St Mary's Priory church at Abergavenny was established at the end of the 11th century by the Norman lord Hamelin de Ballon to support a prior and twelve monks who came from the French Abbey of St Vincent and St Lawrence in Le Mans. It contains the most important collection of tombs in Wales. Alabaster had become popular as an alternative to dark Purbeck 'marble' (which is in fact a shelly limestone)

Fig. 213 Usk. The holy stoup in the west porch

Fig. 214 Abergavenny. Details of the panels from the tomb of Sir William ap Thomas, d.1446, and his wife Gwladys

Fig. 215 Abergavenny. Tomb of Sir Richard Herbert, d.1510

for tomb effigies in the early fourteenth century, and important workshops were established in Nottingham, Lincoln and York within easy reach of quarries in Staffordshire and Derbyshire from which alabaster was extracted. A degree of formalism came with this early example of mass production, and the workshops produced a number of stock designs. This had been seen earlier with the production of encaustic tiles in the thirteenth and fourteenth centuries, identical designs being in evidence at several convents in Wales and elsewhere.

The tomb of Sir Richard Herbert (Fig. 215) is a good example of a late Perpendicular tomb, and the very depressed ogee canopy can be contrasted with the tomb of about 1340 in Brecon Cathedral with its very tall ogee. The depressed arch made room for panel-work beneath. Effigies did not as a rule seek to produce a likeness of the person concerned; they were often produced in workshops to order with their carvers having no knowledge of the persons for which they were intended. The panel which represents Sir Richard's wife flanked by their children kneeling in prayer behind the effigy was also a stock-in-trade of the workshops which produced them. They became common after 1500, and one frequently finds them in Renaissance tombs. But the panels on the side of Sir William ap Thomas's tomb of fifty years earlier show just how full of vigour the sculpture could be (Fig. 214).

Sir William de Hastings died in 1349, and his tomb is an interesting blend of Perpendicular and Decorated (Fig. 216). The arcades consist of quite tall ogees, and the cusping and crockets are elaborate. Behind them there is Perpendicular wall panelling, the cornice carries foliage which is set firmly within squares, and the flamboyant style of the later Decorated period has here been forsaken.

Fig. 216 Abergavenny. Tomb of Sir William de Hastings, d.1349

Fig. 217 Llandaff. Tomb in the north presbytery aisle

The tomb in the north presbytery aisle of Llandaff (Fig. 217) exploits panelling to the full, some of it rather untidy which is most untypical of Perpendicular

Fig. 218 St Dogmael's. A cadaver

work, and this time the effigy has been replaced by a cadaver, a decaying corpse which serves as a reminder to all that this is the way of all flesh. The cadaver was a favourite warning symbol from its appearance in Britain in the early fourteenth century, and it is interesting how similar the design remained throughout the period. Always naked, always with the flesh stretched tightly across the bones, one hand clutches a robe against the crotch, as at St Dogmael's (Fig. 218).

George de Canterlupe, Lord of Abergavenny 1253-1273, has an effigy carved in wood (Fig. 219). Also of wood is a carving of Jesse (Fig. 220). Alabaster again provides the medium for the carving which adorns the tomb of Sir Richard Herbert and his wife (Fig. 221).

Choir Stalls

In 1403, during Owain Glyndŵr's rebellion, Abergavenny suffered badly, and the Benedictine priory was set on fire. A good deal of damage was done to the church, and the choir stalls perhaps give a clue to the extent of this. The north stalls seem to date from the early fourteenth century, when the

Fig. 219 Abergavenny. George de Canterlupe, Lord of Abergavenny 1253-1273

Fig. 220 *Abergavenny. This oak carving of Jesse once formed the base of an elaborate reredos*

Fig. 221 *Abergavenny. Tomb of Sir Richard Herbert of Coldbrook, beheaded 1459,*
and his wife Margaret

church was rebuilt following a rather damning report by the bishop of Hereford who had found that the monks had been neglecting both their Offices and their buildings. They are full of life with their complex flamboyant panels and foliated decorative cornice, but the south stalls are rather more subdued and formal. These probably belong to the early

Figs. 222-224 Abergavenny. Stalls, north side panels (top and centre), south side panels (lower)

156

Fig. 225 Abergavenny. Stalls, north side cornice

fifteenth century, being a replacement for the set which could have been destroyed in the fire. A part of a decorated band in the north stalls has been renewed, and the carving here resembles the work of the south stalls which again indicates a later date for the latter. The misericords of the north stalls have plain rectangular corbels with rounded edges, and the seats are slightly concave, and this type is characteristic of the fourteenth century. Those of the south stalls have polygonal corbels which became fashionable from the late fourteenth century onwards.

The choir stalls in St Davids Cathedral date from about 1500, and the set of misericords is superbly carved. The bishop's throne or cathedra stands next to the south stalls,

Fig. 226 St Davids Cathedral. The choir stalls

and it has very few rivals. Its exact date is unknown, and it has been suggested that remodelling has taken place since it was constructed, which has confused things. The throne features a particular type of canopy which came into fashion in about 1350, and remained in use throughout the rest of the medieval period. Early fourteenth-century canopies often feature tall triangular projections above an ogee head, and the ogee canopy had been fashionable since the 1290s. In the St Davids' throne however the later type resembles the top

two-thirds of a very tall ogee, its sides therefore concave, the canopy at the point of springing being markedly canted inwards. This suggests that the throne dates from after Bishop Gower's episcopate.

The north transept at St Dogmael's was rebuilt in the sixteenth century, and this rebuilding would probably have continued to include the whole of the east end if the dissolution had not come. Shown here are some fragments that remain (Figs. 228-231).

*Fig. 228 St Dogmael's.
The Eagle of St John*

*Fig. 227 St Davids Cathedral.
The cathedra*

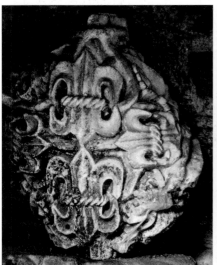

Fig. 229-231 St Dogmael's. Roof bosses. The north transept was rebuilt in the early sixteenth century, and Tudor-period motifs can be seen

At Monmouth, evidence that the abbots and priors were providing rather lavish accommodation for themselves by the end of the monastic period is evidenced by a splendid oriel window (Fig. 232).

St Davids

The Holy Trinity Chapel at St Davids Cathedral was built during the episcopate of Edward Vaughan between 1509 and 1523, and this final building phase at St Davids provides an appropriately serene note on which to end this chapter. Limestone is a welcome guest, and its beautiful warm colouring complements the exquisitely subtle architecture

Fig. 232 Monmouth. Little remains of the Benedictine priory, but this late Perpendicular oriel known as Geoffrey's window (after Geoffrey of Monmouth) survives from the conventual buildings

perfectly. The chapel has been given a fan vault, a type rarely favoured outside Britain, and here the ribs are not separate from the webbing but are now fully integrated into the design both physically and decoratively. The inverted concave-sided cones rise up to meet perfect arcs of circles, and the ribs are all of equal length and profile, these features being the salient characteristics of the true fan vault. Rare Continental examples such as the delightful find in the cloisters of St Stephen's Priory in the Spanish city of Salamanca which also dates from the early sixteenth century lack the

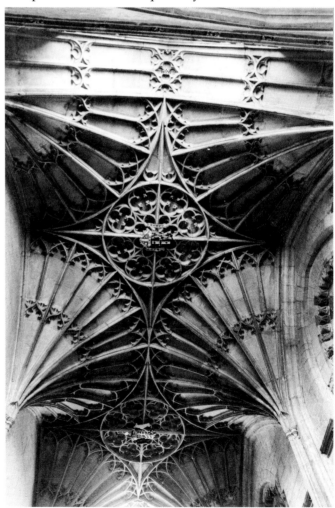

Fig. 233 St Davids Cathedral. The Holy Trinity Chapel vault

Fig. 234 St Davids Cathedral. A screen enclosing the Holy Trinity Chapel

characteristic surface panelling of Perpendicular work in Britain, and the construction technique at St Stephen's is one of separate ribs with an infilling of webbing in a conventional manner. At St Davids the vaulting shafts and capitals are incredibly attenuated, and the burst of activity above is all the more majestic for that. To the north and south the delicate open screens carry a series of bosses on the cornices, and although the carving is exuberant and inventive it is never allowed to stray beyond the confines of its borders, and thereby the lines remain undiluted. The doorways, four-centred, carry mouldings which flow into the tracery of the screens, and all of the lines are soft, and gentle. The chapel quietly sleeps, in an age of peace, brought about by a Welshman's victory at Bosworth field whose coat of arms decorates one of the vault's bosses. It is unaware of what lies just beyond the horizon, during the reign of another Henry.

12

The Dissolution and After

The idea of dissolving the monasteries was not new. During the years around 1520 Cardinal Wolsey and Henry VIII were seriously discussing closing a number of the smaller religious houses and using their endowments and assets to found a series of new cathedrals, something that was not to happen until after the dissolution. In 1524 Wolsey had persuaded the Pope to let him close twenty-nine of the smaller houses so that he could use their assets to finance his founding of a school at Ipswich and a college at Oxford.

King Henry VIII's quarrel with Rome over his matrimonial affairs had led in 1534 to his Act of Supremacy, declaring himself the supreme head of the Church of England after his break with Rome. Another Act of the same year forbade any monk to travel outside the country on business, thus severing connections with Rome and Catholic Europe. A third Act granted the king a further one-tenth of the church's annual income, and this was intended to bolster the exchequer in anticipation of wars with the Catholic monarchs of Europe.

Henry's actions had led to a severing of papal religious authority, and the dissolution of the monasteries, when it came, was swift and comprehensive in both England and Wales. In 1536 Henry ordered the suppression of all religious houses with an annual income of below £200. This was also the year of his First Act of Union, which finally brought Wales completely under the sway of the English throne. In 1539 he ordered the dissolution of all the remaining monasteries representing as they did the personification of Catholicism in Britain, and by 1540 the process was complete. The monasteries were systematically stripped of all their treasures by the king's agents, and there are documented accounts of timber fittings such as choir stalls and parclose screens being used as fire-wood to melt down the lead from the roofs into ingots ready for transportation. Icons were destroyed, the worship of images being a particular characteristic of Catholic ritual. Stained glass was smashed. Stone was taken to be used elsewhere, and the inmates were pensioned off. Some abbots resisted the dissolution and paid with their lives. The systematic destruction of many buildings was a deliberate policy to ensure that the monastic movement could not rise again, but some monastic churches lived on as parish churches, the conventual buildings around them and sometimes also the eastern sections of the church where the monks had sung their Offices being largely destroyed. Examples can be seen at Ewenny, Abergavenny, Beddgelert, Chepstow, Kidwelly, Margam, Penmon, and Usk. St John's Priory church at Brecon became the parish church, and then finally a cathedral in 1923.

There was no general public outcry against the king's actions against the religious houses, and this was a reflection of the state of the relationship between monastery and lay-society at the time. For several generations before the dissolution there had been an increasing trend towards patronising the church at parish level rather than at monastic and cathedral level, this being reflected in the flowering of late Perpendicular parish church architecture in many places, good examples including Mold, Wrexham, and Cardiff. The monastery had been a part of the fabric of life for hundreds of years, no one living more than about an hour's walk away from an abbey or a cathedral in lowland areas. Yet when the dissolution came it seems to have been received with something of a universal shrug of the shoulders. This must reflect the fact that the closure of the monasteries brought to a sudden end an institution which was drifting towards a natural extinction anyway. It also reflected the increasing secularization of church appointments, something which had been going on since the late fourteenth century. Bishops, abbots and the higher clergy were being chosen from men of learning who would be useful politically and diplomatically, and temporal considerations were outweighing the spiritual. These men therefore had no particular disposition towards the religious houses when the dissolution came, and indeed they often acquiesced. Just before the dissolution there had been localized uprisings in the north of England (the Pilgrimage of Grace), Cornwall and Ireland, these being to do with grievances among lay-communities as much as with an attempted opposition to the closure of religious houses, and a delegation of abbots and laymen sent to the king from the north was promptly imprisoned in the Tower of London and its members executed. The other uprisings were dealt with just as swiftly and brutally.

There were very few dissenters in Wales. Those few that did included John Davies who had left Wales in order to pursue an austere monastic life as a member of the Carthusian Order, and he and other Carthusians were starved to death in Newgate prison having refused to take the Oath of Supremacy. John Eynon, a secular priest who served the abbot of Reading, was martyred with him after refusing to surrender his parish to the authorities. Edward Powell, a scholar educated at Oxford in the service of the king who had been ordered to publish a reply to Martin Luther's writings and polemic, was sent to the Tower of London and executed in 1540 after refusing to take the Oath of Succession.

In Scotland, the dissolution was rather more gradual, some monasteries surviving into the seventeenth century albeit in a somewhat truncated form, and on the Continent of Europe it did not disappear completely. The monasteries were seen as having departed almost completely from their original ideals of poverty and devout living, whilst their work as educators had largely been eclipsed. Even the friars, who had kept to their original ideals more closely than had the other Orders, were no longer as vital a part of the universities as they had once been. The Orders had outlived their usefulness, and change was in the air. There were numerous accounts of the decay to which some monastic buildings had fallen into already, but what the dissolution caused was the swift destruction of many of the greatest buildings that the country has ever seen.

The Reformation and after

Henry VIII's Act of Union in 1536 created the Church of England in Wales. The next two hundred years were characterized by a general demoralization and a decline in respect given to the established church by the English, but even more so by the Welsh. The starting point was the way in which Catholicism was reinstated by Queen Mary, accompanied by some three hundred Protestant martyrs including Bishop Robert Ferrar of St Davids, and then banished again by Queen Elizabeth I who also replaced virtually all the bishops in Wales and England. Such switches in doctrine at the whim of successive monarchs did not bode well for the established church's credibility, and it was now plain that the church was no longer the political force that it had once been. During the first decade of the sixteenth century the public gave over £80,000 to the church, but during the last decade it gave less than £2,000. In Elizabeth's long reign thirteen of the sixteen bishops appointed to the four ancient sees of Wales were Welshmen, but this trend did not continue. The English absentee bishop became the norm rather than the exception, and the Welsh bishoprics came to be used as stepping stones on the way to the rich dioceses of England. By the time of the Georgian period this can be clearly seen. George I appointed six bishops to Welsh sees, and before he died all except one were translated to English sees. George II appointed twenty bishops, fifteen of whom he translated to English sees. George III appointed twenty-three, eleven subsequently being translated. George IV appointed five, translating one before his death. Between 1714 and 1870 none of the Welsh bishops were Welsh speakers.

One reaction to this centrally imposed English hierarchy was the rise of Nonconformism, another was the desire for the Bible and service books to be in Welsh, just as the English had reacted to the use of Latin from the 1370s onwards.

William Salesbury (c.1520-c.1584) was a scholar from Llansannan, Conwy. He was educated at Oxford, and in 1547 produced an English-Welsh dictionary. In 1567 he translated into Welsh the English Book of Common Prayer, and he was also the principal translator of the New Testament into Welsh. In 1588 Dr William Morgan, a vicar and scholar who was to become bishop of Llandaff in 1595 and of St Asaph in 1601, brought out a translation from the Greek and Hebrew of the whole bible which included a revision of Salesbury's new testament. In 1620 Dr Richard Parry, bishop of St Asaph, assisted by his chaplain, Dr John Davies, published a revised edition which is virtually the same as the present Authorized Translation.

Such welcome activities were being accompanied by other somewhat less savoury practices which were to characterize the decline of the established church for the next few centuries. In 1587 John Penry was campaigning against the growing practices of the appropriations of church revenues and resources to favoured relatives and colleagues of the higher clergy who did not have any connections with the Welsh church. For instance, Bishop Hughes of St Asaph was found to have appropriated to himself sixteen of the richest livings in commendam (that is in trust to him), and most of the other rich livings were in possession of those who lived out of the Principality. Penry's publication of a pamphlet drawing attention to the spiritual destitution of Wales, which he addressed to Queen Elizabeth and Parliament, drew attention to the fact that non-resident clergymen were the rule rather than the exception, and in the diocese of St Asaph, for instance, only three of the incumbents were in fact resident in their parishes: 'Thousands of our people know Jesus Christ to be neither God nor man, priest nor prophet, almost never heard of Him ... Preaching in many parts is quite unknown. In some places a sermon is read once in three months.' Penry can not have expected his exposures to have been welcomed with open arms, but nor could he have fully anticipated the reaction that did come. His pamphlet was seized, and he was arrested. Archbishop John Whitgift, a close associate of Queen Elizabeth who shared her hatred of Puritans, succeeded in getting a law onto the statute books in 1593 making Puritanism an offence, and in that year Penry was martyred at the early age of thirty-three. It could be said that the seeds of the Welsh Nonconformist Movement were thus sown.

In 1621 the reverend John Edwards, a well-known clergymen of his day, confessed that barely one in fifteen clergymen in Wales spoke Welsh, and during the next decade a number of clergymen were removed from office for raising similar concerns. Vavasor Powell (1617-70) was a Welsh Nonconformist Puritan, and an itinerate preacher in Wales who was twice arrested for his activities. But during the English Civil War he went to preach in and around London, and after Cromwell's victory he returned to Wales with a 'certificate of character'. When in 1650 parliament appointed a commission for the better propagation and preaching of the gospel in Wales, Powell was one of its principal advisers. But when the Restoration of the Monarchy in 1660 brought to the throne in Charles II a Catholic monarch who dared not proclaim his faith openly, Powell was imprisoned for seven years. After a year's freedom, he was again imprisoned and died soon after.

William of Orange, perhaps the first English monarch who could be called a Protestant unequivocally, passed the Act of Toleration in 1689. Nonconformist churches began to be built instead of the meeting places disguised as houses, and within fifteen years of the Act about 40,000 bibles in Welsh were distributed. In 1730 the Great Methodist Revival began, and it saw a series of prominent evangelists emerge including Griffith Jones, rector of Llanddowror, Daniel Rowland of Llangeitho, and Howell Harries of Trevecca, the founder of Calvinistic Methodism. Griffith Jones ministered for fifty-three years under nine successive English-speaking bishops of St Davids who had little to do with their predominantly Welsh-speaking see, and in the 1730s he established a series of Circulating Schools. He believed that children could be taught much of the basics of education in a relatively short, intense period of study, and then the teachers would move on to the next school for a similar teaching period there. He died in 1761, leaving £7,000 to fund their continuation, but Bridget Bevan, the original trustee, died and his will was not carried out. The schools collapsed in 1779, but in 1809 the legacy had grown to £30,000, and Madam Bevan's Charity was established to continue the work.

In the nineteenth century the state to which the church buildings themselves had descended was receiving notice. The Report of the Welsh Clergy of West Riding in Yorkshire in 1852 stated:

> Some of the members of your Committee have both witnessed and deplored the dilapidated state of the churches in the diocese of St Davids. They have seen churches entirely deserted by the parishioners, some of them without doors, converted into lodging places for sheep and cattle, and others without roofs, admitting the rains of heaven freely into the interior: the books, communion plate, and surplices having

disappeared, and nowhere to be found, the performance of divine service therein having ceased for many years. Yea, in some of the localities the churches themselves have entirely disappeared, leaving only the name to mark their site.

This gathering in Yorkshire of clergy of Welsh descent had from 1821 published annual reports on the state to which the established church was descending, and they were for instance partitioning against the proposed merging of the dioceses of Bangor and St Asaph to divert funds to help found the new see of Manchester. The Association of Welsh Clergy in the West Riding of Yorkshire was officially founded in 1835, and that same year saw them petitioning the prime minister over Welsh bishoprics being filled by English monoglots.

The annual report of 1852 refers also to a general misappropriation of funds. A further report of 1854 draws attention to some goings on in the diocese of Llandaff:

> The Prebend of Langwm, value £84 4s.6d., has been held since 1813 by the Rev. Richard Watson (son of Bishop Watson), an Englishman, who was also appointed to the Registrar-ship of the diocese when he was *five years old*, [the report's italics] and he has now held it for 60 years, and has received from it altogether upwards of £40,000. The Bishop also got him appointed when he was eight years of age to the Registrar-ship of the Diocese of London, which he has now held for 57 years, and from which he has received upwards of £27,720.

Many other instances are cited in Wales and England.

All this fuelled the Nonconformist movement in Britain, and in Wales there was the added factor of the English absentee bishop. By 1800 there were well over a hundred Nonconformist chapels in Wales, and by 1900 there were more than two thousand. The chapel or Welsh *capel* had taken the place of the Anglican church in the spiritual lives of the Welsh, and Catholic emancipation in 1829 provided a further alternative to the Church of England. Pressures to disestablish the Anglican church came also from the fact that tithes and other dues were still being paid to an institution whose support was dwindling. If it were to survive in Wales, a church of the Anglican doctrine would have to sever its formal ties with England and rebuild in its stead an institution that had its mission and heart unequivocally in the Principality. In 1920 it was disestablished and disendowed, to be replaced by the *Church in Wales*, so ending over eight hundred years of English domination. Anglican in doctrine but autonomous, it is fully independent of both the state and of the Church of England. Like all Anglican churches however, it recognises the primacy of the Archbishop of Canterbury. It may have been expected that St Davids would at last have become the metropolitan see, but it was decided that the seat of the archbishop would rotate among the six dioceses, each incumbent holding the office for the duration of his own tenure as bishop.

Two new sees were set up, that of Swansea and Brecon in 1923, for which the former Benedictine priory of Brecon was chosen as the cathedral; and Newport, Monmouth and Gwent, for which St Woolos at Newport was chosen. The latter was not an automatic choice. Many other buildings were considered, and the renovation of Tintern Abbey was even seriously mooted. St Woolos, the pro-cathedral since disestablishment, was finally confirmed as the cathedral in 1949, its geographical position at the heart of the diocese being a deciding factor. It is the only cathedral in Britain which incorporates pre-Norman work in its fabric above ground level substantial enough to be called a structure, and thus a material link with the Celtic past has remained.

Appendix 1

Stonemasons' Marks

The medieval stonemason served a seven-year apprenticeship, and initially there was a strong tradition of the craft being perpetuated from father to son, an apprentice usually beginning at the age of thirteen or fourteen. By the end of the thirteenth century the more modern kind of apprenticeship is recognisable, whereby many of the apprentices were no longer trained by members of their own family. After this training period the mason would spend several years travelling as a jobbing mason, and this was regarded as an essential part of his education, bringing him into contact as it did with a variety of building types, methods of construction, and points of style. The masons' marks, which can be seen in many places throughout the fabric of medieval buildings, are mainly the legacy of this latter phase of the mason's training, and they were used as signs of identification since a mason was often paid on a piece-work basis. The signs appear usually upon plain blocks of dressed stone or simple mouldings, and a team of masons would be employed to turn these out in quantity, sometimes at the quarry, sometimes at the site of the building. The signs are generally neatly inscribed with the aid of a straight edge, and curving lines are relatively uncommon.

One would expect to find a collection of similar marks appearing in several buildings, conjuring up visions of a team of masons moving from job to job, but in fact such collections are extremely rare. It is usual to find only one or two similar signs which are common to two or more buildings, if one finds any at all, and the picture is somewhat confused by the presence of very similar signs appearing on buildings which are known to have been built generations apart. Only the more complicated marks can be ascribed to one particular mason with any confidence, the very simple signs such as arrows, crosses and stars cropping up regularly throughout the period. The more complex signs would sometimes be the result of an accumulation of additions throughout successive generations of a family of stonemasons.

The master mason's mark would never appear. He did not dress stone, and the more complex carving would be done by fully trained masons who were paid either for the job or on a per day basis, and so marks here were not necessary. It turns out then that masons' marks tell us little about the buildings themselves beyond an indication of which parts were erected at the same time, and even where several types appear at, say, two locations this implies nothing about the architect — the master mason who actually designed the building, for a single master would not necessarily have been associated with both buildings at all.

The marks illustrated are not drawn to a uniform scale, but generally the palm of the hand will just cover a complete mark. At AbbeyCwmhir there are quite a variety of marks which suggests the employment of a large team of masons to build this enormous nave, the largest in Wales. The same goes for Montgomery Castle (Henry III would have wanted it built as quickly as possible) and Margam Abbey, both these sets of marks being complex. St Davids' presbytery was built after the nave, and contains a different set of marks as a result. At Asaph Cathedral the nave took a long time to build, and the different set of marks present in the north and the south arcades reflects the fact.

Presteigne parish church, nave arcade, *c*.1200

Llanthony Abbey, last quarter of twelfth century

Brecon Cathedral transepts, second quarter of thirteenth century

AbbeyCwmhir, *c*.1220

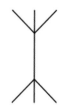   

Valle Crucis Abbey, early thirteenth century

Montgomery Castle, 1223-27

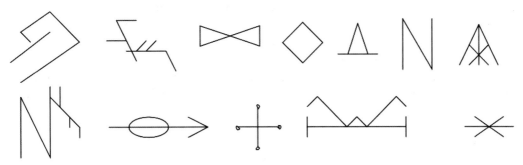

Margam Abbey, early thirteenth-century ruins

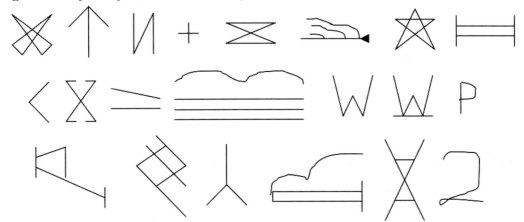

St Davids Cathedral: nave, last quarter of twelfth century

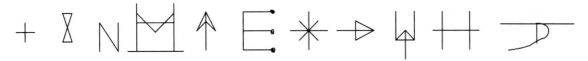

Presbytery, early thirteenth century

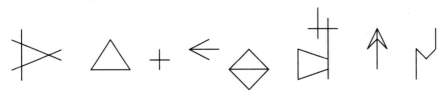

Neath Abbey: church, 1280-1330

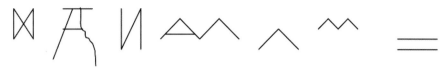

Brecon Cathedral, nave, *c*.1300-40

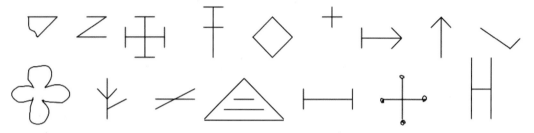

St Asaph Cathedral, nave, fourteenth century, north arcade

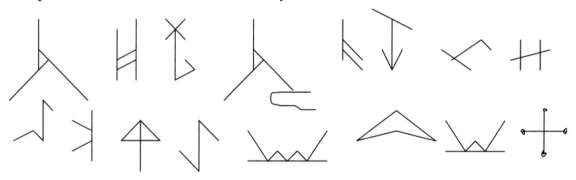

South arcade

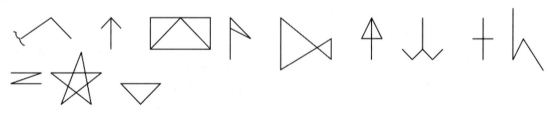

Crossing

Appendix 2

Other Monastic Sites

The focus of this book has been upon the architecture and the institutions that brought it into being, and for this reason a number of foundations where there are little or no remains, some of which played an important part in the religious life of Wales, have received scant or no mention. Here then follows a brief summary of these, a number of which lacked both the resources and the number of incumbents to justify building on anything like the scale of the larger abbeys and priories.

Benedictine Houses

Cardigan had a small Benedictine cell, the origins of which are obscure. It was probably founded in about 1100 by Gilbert de Clare as a cell of Gloucester Abbey, but when Rhys ap Gruffudd regained Cardigan from the Normans it was re-founded by him, becoming a cell of St Peter's Abbey in Chertsey, Surrey. It is first mentioned in this context in a charter of 1165. The cell never housed more than two or three monks throughout its life, and they made use of the chancel of the existing parish church.

 Goldcliff was founded close to the mouth of the river Usk, and by the end of the fifteenth century the monastery had ceased to function and some of its buildings had already been claimed by the sea. An existing church had been given to the abbey of Bec in France by Robert de Chandos, the local Norman ruler, in about 1113. Its endowments lay largely in Somerset however, both this and its alien status creating difficulties in later years. Its holdings were considerably reduced in the fourteenth century following a dispute between the abbot and the then patron Philip de Columbers, and again when a monk of Tintern Abbey, bearing a forged papal bull, succeeded in becoming prior. The latter had a personal patron in Sir John Inge of Somerset, who proceeded to relieve the priory of more of its possessions.

 Monmouth Priory was founded by Guihenoc of Monmouth in about 1100, a daughter house of St Florent near Saumur in France. As an alien priory it suffered difficulties in the fourteenth century, but in the fifteenth it became independent of its French abbey, now coming under the jurisdiction of God's House College, Cambridge. By the dissolution the church was apparently in very poor condition, the present church being a modern structure which abuts the medieval tower. This tower, to the west of the nave, reflects the fact that an existing parish church was adapted for monastic use.

Llangennith Priory in Glamorgan was a small cell of the abbey of St Taurinus in Normandy, founded early in the twelfth century by Richard Earl of Warwick. The monks worshipped in the chancel of the parish church. An alien priory, it was granted by Henry VI to All Souls College, Oxford in 1441.

Cistercian Houses

Strata Marcella near Welshpool was founded by Owain Cyfelliog, Prince of Powys, in 1170, and continued to be patronised by his descendents. However, early in the fourteenth century the local English magnate John Charleton succeeded in supplanting the Welsh community with English monks and the house came under the administration of Buildwas Abbey. It suffered during the rebellion of Owain Glyndŵr as a result.

Llansantffraed in Elfael was established as a daughter house of Strata Marcella in 1170, the first house of Cistercian nuns in Wales. Apparently the first abbot of Strata Marcella eloped with one of the nuns, and this short-lived convent seems never to have recovered from the incident.

Llanllyr, the second Cistercian nunnery in Wales, was founded near Aberaeron as a daughter house of Strata Florida in about 1180, and it is possible that some of the nuns came from Llansantffraed in Elfael. It was regarded as a small cell of Strata Florida, and on the death of The Lord Rhys, its founder, Strata Florida took over some of its lands.

Llanllugan, north of Newtown, had a Cistercian nunnery which was founded in about 1200 by Maredudd ap Rhotpert, Lord of Cydewain. The house was not well endowed, and this small establishment made use of a church to the north of the site of the convent. The presence of a medieval font in this church, something never seen in Cistercian houses, confirms the building's use as a parish church which was also used by the small community of nuns.

Conwy II began life at Rhedynog Felen near Caernarvon, but soon moved to Conwy where some remains of the church's west front are incorporated into the present parish church. This establishment is conveniently known as Conwy I. It was patronised by the Welsh rulers and was granted large areas of land in Snowdonia, but with the coming of Edward I the community had to be moved, and in 1284 the king provided for their relocation to Maenan, known as Conwy II, a few miles to the south.

Whitland was founded by the French abbey of Clairvaux in 1140, but the Welsh soon took it in hand, and it was patronised by The Lord Rhys, ruler of the reinvigorated kingdom of Deheubarth. Its history was blighted by a combination of destruction and plundering particularly during the wars of Edward I and Owain Glyndŵr, and also poor management throughout its existence; and despite being an important Cistercian house from which Strata Florida, Strata Marcella and AbbeyCwmhir were founded, its own state seems to have been one of continuing troubles.

Llantarnam Abbey was founded by Hywel ap Iorwerth in about 1179, a daughter house of Strata Florida. Unlike other monasteries in the Anglo-Norman dominated south, Llantarnam was a house with strong Welsh allegiances. During the Glyndŵr rebellion abbot John ap Hywel was killed by the English whilst taking part in the fighting at Usk.

Grace Dieu near Monmouth was a small, troubled and impoverished community. After its founding by John, Lord of Monmouth in 1226 it was completely destroyed in 1233 by Llywelyn the Great. Relocation west of Monmouth brought more peaceful times but again during the Welsh wars later in the thirteenth century there was considerable destruction. The precise location of any subsequent rebuilding is not known.

Augustinian Houses

Bardsey island off the Lleyn peninsular, known to the Welsh as Ynys Enlli and reputed to be the burial place of 20,000 saints, was an ancient Celtic foundation which adopted the Augustinian order in about 1200. It held much land in the Lleyn peninsular, but was never a large or prosperous house.

Small priory cells existed on **St Tudwal's** island and at **St Kynemark** near Chepstow. Little is known of either, both having been ancient Celtic foundations which had adopted the Augustinian Order in the thirteenth century.

Haverfordwest Priory was founded by Robert FitzRichard shortly before 1200, and

Fig. 235 Haverfordwest. The priory's gardens have recently been recreated by Cadw

it seems to have lived an uneventful life with little evidence of rebuilding activity for some time after the initial building phase. In the 1990s extensive excavation work carried out by Cadw revealed that in the mid-fifteenth century the main cloister area and the chapter house were rebuilt, and to the east of the latter an elaborate grid pattern consisting of low stone walls was laid out for the cultivation of flower and herb gardens. Medieval references and illustrations of gardens are numerous, and in many cases the cloister garth of the convent was used for this purpose. At Haverfordwest, advantage was taken of the extensive area of land between the eastern conventual buildings and the river for their laying out. Justification for the cultivation of flowers in a monastery was provided for instance by the descriptions in *The Song of Songs* of beautiful gardens, symbolizing a virgin bride and hence the Virgin Mary. This is an ancient book containing more or less explicit references to love in its various manifestations which has received numerous translations and interpretations during the last two thousand years. A sixteenth-century document records that Prior Thomas Rogers rented a room above the church with its associated area of garden to a friar.

Carmarthen Priory was originally a Celtic foundation which became a Benedictine cell of Battle Abbey during the reign of Henry I. It did not prosper, and it was re-founded soon after as an Augustinian house by Bishop Bernard of St Davids in 1125 and given endowments which placed it on a more secure financial footing. Suffering much damage during the rebellion of Owain Glyndŵr, it apparently recovered and prospered until the dissolution.

Premonstatensian Houses

Talley Abbey in Carmarthenshire, the only abbey of this Order in Wales, was founded by the Lord Rhys ap Gruffyd some time during the 1180s. It was never prosperous, and its buildings were not completed to the original plan. The nave for instance as finished was of only four bays, and the north aisle was never completed. After the death of Rhys, Abbot Peter attempted to get the house converted to the Cistercian Order in the hope that it could become a dependency of Whitland Abbey as a way of improving its financial situation. A petition by the displaced canons to Canterbury reversed Peter's actions but he managed to hold on to some of Talley's endowments, leading to its further impoverishment. In 1278 it had to be taken into royal custody, and was placed in the care of Welbeck Abbey.

Cluniac Houses

Malpas Priory near Newport was founded by Winibald of Caerleon early in the twelfth century as a daughter house of Montacute in Somerset. As a Cluniac house it was deemed an alien priory, and in 1339 Edward III severed its connections with Cluny via its mother house and its tithes were granted to William, Earl of Salisbury, Marshal of England.

St Clear's Priory in Carmarthenshire was founded some time between 1147 and 1184, as a daughter house of St Martin de Champs in Paris. It never prospered, never more than a prior and two monks being recorded at any one time and who made use of the parish church. In 1414 it was dissolved as an alien priory.

Houses of Friars

Apart from at Brecon, Dominican friaries were established at Bangor, Rhuddlan, Haverfordwest and Cardiff.

The **Bangor** house was established in the thirteenth century, and dissolved in 1538. The site was bought by Geoffrey Glyn who bequeathed it for the establishment of a school. This was formally established by Elizabeth I in 1561, and the Friars School continues today.

Rhuddlan was founded in the thirteenth century before Edward I conquered north Wales, and when he laid out the plan of the new town of Rhuddlan it left the friary isolated from the urban centre where the friars normally preferred to be. Fragments of the cloister are incorporated in a modern farm building called Plas-newydd.

Franciscan friaries were established at Llanfaes, Carmarthen and Cardiff.

Llanfaes was founded by Llewelyn ap Iorwerth (Llewelyn the Great) to house the tomb of his wife Joan, an illegitimate daughter of King John. It was consecrated in 1240. After the dissolution the church was used as a barn until finally being pulled down in the nineteenth century.

One of the largest friaries in Britain, **Carmarthen** was founded in the late thirteenth century, probably by Edward I. It was the original burial place of Edmund Tudor, father of Henry VII.

Newport had a community of Austin friars, the only example of this Order in Wales. It was a comparatively late foundation, established by Hugh, second Earl of Stafford in 1377. The site is now occupied by Newport Bus Station.

Glossary

Abacus.	A thin plate of stone which sits between a capital and an arch.
Abbey.	A convent which is ruled over by an abbot or abbess.
Ambulatory.	A walkway behind the high altar which connects the north and south presbytery aisles.
Annulet.	A decorative (or sometimes supportive) ring around a shaft.
Apse.	A polygonal or semicircular termination for an aisle, presbytery etc.
Arcade.	A series of arches. A blind arcade is built against a wall such that there is no access through the archways.
Ashlar.	Stone which has been hewn to form regular smooth blocks for wall facings.
Aumbry.	Wall cupboard or recess for storing Communion vessels.
Ballflower.	Decorative motif consisting of a bulbous form in the top of which is incised a trefoil to give the appearance of opening petals. Characteristic of the later Decorated period.
Bar tracery.	Window tracery formed with a series of skeletal ribs or bars.
Batter.	Name given to the bottom section of a wall if it is splayed outwards or inclined.
Battlement.	A parapet with a series of rectangular or square open gaps cut into it.
Bay.	Vertical division of an elevation, inside or outside, marked by buttresses, fenestration, beams, arches etc.
Billet.	Decorative motif used in Romanesque architecture consisting of a line of small rectangular projections which are separated by spaces of similar width.
Blindstorey.	The space of walling, sometimes decorated, between the main arcade of arches and the clerestory.
Boss.	Block of stone (or timber) covering the joints between the ribs of a vault or ceiling.
Broach spire.	A spire with a hexagonal base which rests directly on top of rather than within the walls of a tower, the diagonal faces carrying small attached spirelets or *broaches* to fill the corners.
Buttress.	A mass of stone which is built out from a wall to lend additional support.
Cable moulding.	A moulding imitating the appearance of twisted cord.
Came.	Metal strip which supports the individual panes of a stained glass window.
Capital.	Block of stone above a column which supports an arch or vaulting springer.
Cathedra.	Bishop's throne.
Cathedral.	Bishop's church.
Centring.	Timber supports for arches and vaults during construction.
Chancel.	Eastern part of a church which contains the high altar.
Chantry chapel.	Chapel inside or built against a church which is endowed for the celebration of mass for its founder.

Chapter house.	Place of assembly in a convent or cathedral for the discussion of business.
Chevet.	A semicircular or polygonal ambulatory with a number of radiating chapels.
Chevron.	Zig-zag motif characteristic of the Norman period.
Clerestory.	In church architecture, the windows high above the main arcade. It can also be applied to high windows above a section of walling in secular architecture.
Cloister.	An enclosed space; in a convent it is provided with covered walkways which connect the various conventual buildings.
Compound pier.	A pier with a number of shafts or elements.
Convent.	A community of monks, nuns, canons regular or friars.
Corbel.	Projecting member which supports a vault, beam etc.
Corbel arch.	An arch formed by overlapping corbels which progressively reach across from each wall.
Corbel table.	A row of corbels, supporting a parapet etc.
Cornice.	Projecting ornamental band at the top of a wall, screen, etc.
Crenellation.	Same as battlements.
Crocket.	Decorative flamboyant feature projecting from the sides of canopies, pinnacles and the like.
Crown.	Top or apex of an arch or vault.
Cusp.	Projecting point in the head of an arch, window opening etc.
Dagger.	Decorative motif consisting of a trefoil-cusped lancet which tapers towards a point at the bottom.
Depressed arch.	An arch whose height is less than half of its span.
Detached shaft.	Free-standing shaft supported at the top and the bottom; sometimes also supported at intervals along its length.
Dogtooth.	Decorative motif consisting of a square-based pyramid with a V groove incised into each face to form a projecting cross pattern, characteristic of the Early English period.
Dressed stone.	Stone which has been regularly shaped, with smooth surfaces.
Engaged shaft.	A shaft which has been let into the wall such that only a part (usually half) of its surface is visible.
Falsework.	Timber supports for walls, towers etc during construction.
Fenestration.	The aesthetic contribution of the windows to a building.
Finial.	Foliated ornament at the top of a pinnacle, canopy etc.
Flying Buttress.	A semi-arch which leans against a wall to lend support.
Friary.	A convent of friars.
Gargoyle.	A waterspout which has been decorated with grotesque carving.
Grotesque.	Decorative member embellishing the exterior (or interior) walls of a building, featuring creatures or human forms.
Hood-mould.	Projecting moulding above an opening to throw off the rain water. Also used decoratively internally.
Impost.	Projecting member like a corbel on which an arch rests.
Jamb.	The vertical inner face of an archway, door or window opening.
Keel moulding.	A narrow moulding along a shaft, string-course etc which resembles the keel of a boat.
Keystone.	The top, central stone of an arch or vault.
Label.	Same as hood-mound.
Label-stop.	Termination for a hood-mould.

Lancet.	Pointed, slender opening.
Lantern tower.	Tower in which the windows are allowed to light the interior as seen from below.
Lierne vault.	A vault with additional short decorative ribs or *liernes* which span the main structural ribs.
Loop.	Small narrow opening, as in a stair turret or a defensive wall.
Misericord.	Tip-up seat in choir stalls which can be used as a ledge to sit upon such that one still appears to be standing, often carved with entertaining scenes. Also the name given to a chamber in a convent near the farmery where it was permitted to eat meat.
Monastery.	A convent for monks.
Mouchette.	Dagger motif with a curling blade.
Moulding.	Carving applied to a projecting member such as an arch order, string-course etc.
Mullion.	Vertical member which divides windows and other openings into separate compartments.
Narthex.	Canopy, porch or antechamber before the west door of a church, common in Cistercian houses.
Nave.	The western arm of a church.
Newel stair.	Spiral staircase, usually built into a turret.
Nook-shaft.	Shaft let into the angle where two wall surfaces meet.
Nunnery.	A convent for nuns.
Ogee.	Profile formed from a stretched out S curve leaning 45 degrees to the left against a mirror image of itself. A double ogee opening consists of an ogee with an inverted ogee immediately below it.
Oratory.	Small private chapel.
Order.	One of a number of concentric bands of decoration around an arch, doorway or window.
Parapet.	Upper section of walling behind which one can stand on a ledge or platform, giving protection from the sheer drop.
Parapet spire.	A spire whose base sits entirely within the confines of a tower's parapet.
Parclose screen.	Screen separating choir, transepts, chapels etc from the main body of the church to afford a degree of privacy.
Pier.	Vertical member which either supports an arch or forms the mass of masonry between arch openings.
Pilaster.	Shallow rectangular buttress.
Pinnacle.	Spirelet which acts as a stabilizing mass.
Piscina.	Niche with a bowl and drain, used for washing Communion vessels.
Plate tracery.	Window tracery formed by visually piercing shapes through solid plates of stone.
Pointing.	Exposed strips of mortar between blocks of masonry or bricks.
Poppyhead.	Decorative foliated finial with Fleur-de-lis or similar pattern.
Presbytery.	Part of the church which lies east of the choir.
Priory.	A convent which is ruled over by a prior or prioress.
Pulpitum.	Solid screen which separates the choir from the nave.
Putlog.	Horizontal beam onto which a platform can rest during the construction of a wall.
Putlog hole.	Hole in a wall into which a putlog is inserted.
Quoin.	Block of dressed stone at the corner of a building.
Relieving arch.	Arch built into a wall above an opening which helps to support the weight of the walling above.
Reredos.	Wall or screen behind an altar.

Respond.	A half-pier set against a section of walling which supports an arch, eg at the ends of an arcade.
Reticulated tracery.	Window tracery with repeated patterns.
Retrochoir.	Area east of the presbytery behind the high altar.
Reveal.	The part of a jamb between the window or door and the inner wall surface. If it is shaped diagonally it is called a splay.
Ridge rib.	A rib which runs along the apex of a vault parallel to the side walls.
Rood.	A crucifix, usually flanked by St Mary the Virgin and St John the Evangelist, set upon a screen or in a loft at the eastern end of the nave.
Sanctuary.	That part of the church which houses the high altar.
Sedilia.	Set of seats for the clergy, normally positioned against the south wall of the presbytery.
Segmental arch.	An arch with its lowest section cut off such that it springs from an angle rather than vertically.
Soffit.	Usually the name given to the underside of an arch, but it can equally apply to the underside of any projecting member.
Spandrel.	Area of walling between and above arch openings.
Splay.	See reveal.
Squint.	Diagonal piercing in a wall through which the high altar can be viewed from transepts, chapels, nave aisles etc.
Stoup.	Bowl to contain holy water next to the entrance of a church.
String-course.	Horizontal projecting decorative strip.
Tierceron vault.	A vault carrying additional structural ribs or *tiercerons* which spring from the same place as the main ribs but meet the ridge rib or other supplementary ribs at oblique angles.
Tracery.	Ornamental pattern work in panelling and in the head of a window.
Transepts.	The north and south arms of a church.
Transom.	Horizontal member in a window or other opening which divides it up into panels.
Tribune.	Gallery stage of an elevation between the main arcade and the clerestory, pierced or arcaded, to give access to the aisle roof behind it.
Triforium.	Blind-storey stage of an elevation between the main arcade and the clerestory, essentially a decorated band of walling; it does not therefore give light or access to the aisle roof void behind it.
Tympanum.	Semicircular (or pointed) panel above a door which fills the space between it and an arch.
Vault.	An arched ceiling of stone or timber, solid rather than open.
Voussoir.	One of the stones or bricks, often wedge shaped, which forms an arch or a vault.

Bibliography

An illustrated guide to the Ancient Monuments of Wales. (HMSO 1973).

Braun, H. *Cathedral Architecture*. (Faber and Faber, 1972).

Butler, L. and Given-Wilson, C. *Medieval Monasteries of Great Britain*. (Michael Joseph, 1983).

Clifton-Taylor, A. *The Cathedrals of England*. (Thames and Hudson, 1967).

Cooper, R.N. *Abbeys and Priories of Wales*. (Christopher Davies, 1992).

Coppack, G. *Abbeys and Priories*. (Batsford/English Heritage, 1990).

Davies, D. (Rev). *The Ancient Celtic Church in Wales*. (Federation of Evangelical Free Churches in Wales, 1910).

Gilyard-Beer, R. *Abbeys*. (HMSO 1958).

Harvey, J. *The Medieval Architect*. (Wayland, 1972).
    English Medieval Architects, a Biographical Dictionary down to 1550. (Alan Sutton, 1987).

Hilling, J.B. *The Historic Architecture of Wales*. (University of Wales Press, 1976).

Little, B. *Architecture in Norman Britain*. (Batsford, 1985).

Morris, R. *Cathedrals and Abbeys of England and Wales*. (Dent, 1979).

Redknap, M. *The Christian Celts, Treasures of Late Celtic Wales*. (National Museum of Wales, 1991).

Robson, P.A. *Saint Davids, the Cathedral and See*. (Bell, 1901).

Soden, R.W. *A Guide to Welsh Parish Churches*. (Gomer, 1984).

Tatton-Brown, T. *Great Cathedrals of Britain*. (BBC, 1989).

Thurlby, M. *Romanesque Architecture and Sculpture in Wales*. (Logaston, 2006).

Williams, D.H. *The Welsh Cistercians*. (Two volumes, Caldey Island 1984).
    Atlas of Cistercian Lands in Wales. (University of Wales Press, 1990).
    White Monks in Gwent and the Border. (The Griffin Press, 1976).

Williams, G. *The Welsh Church from Conquest to Reformation*. (University of Wales Press, 1962).

Williams, R. *Limekilns and Lime-burning*. (Shire, 1989).

Wright, G.N. *Discovering Abbeys and Priories*. (Shire, 1979).

Yarwood, D. *The Architecture of Britain*. (Batsford, 1976).

Yerburgh, D.S. *Tour of the Abbeys, Priories and Cathedrals of Wales, an Itinerant's Exhibition*. (Revd Canon David Yerburgh, Salisbury, 1999).

Index